# A Guide To Seville

## Five Walking Tours

## P S Quick

ACORN BOOKS

Published in 2017 by
Acorn Books
www.acornbooks.co.uk

Acorn Books is an imprint of
Andrews UK Limited
www.andrewsuk.com

Photo credits:
*Plaza del Triunfo* courtesy of José Luis Filpo Cabana
*Consulado de Francia* courtesy of Anual
*Plaza Nueva* courtesy of Anual
*Museo de Bellas Artes de Sevilla* courtesy of Anual
*Calle Betis* courtesy of Zeier Gregory

# Contents

# Introduction

Seville is one of the most charming cities in Spain with its favourable climate and relaxed atmosphere. It is steeped in history and has a unique Moorish heritage that bequeaths the city a large collection of interesting buildings as well as those that are a legacy of the Ibero-American Exhibition of 1929. These five walks give the tourist an opportunity to visit and enjoy not only the major attractions that a guided tour usually includes but also many of the other interesting sights that people do not always see.

This book will help you experience the atmosphere of different areas in Seville with its gardens, palaces, religious institutions, museums and other buildings, transporting you back through time by walking through the smaller streets and hidden plazas that have a historical and cultural significance with their blend of architectural styles. By providing five different walking routes and detailed information about each attraction passed it puts a visitor to Seville in charge of the time spent at any particular place rather than having to rush and keep up with a guide. With detailed instructions of how to get from one place to another it gives a flavour of the many things that Seville has to offer without having to join costly guided tours.

# Preparation

- Seville has a wonderful climate with very mild winters but the summers can be intensely hot. Plan the time of your visit according to the activities you want to experience. If you visit in the height of summer you will need to escape the sun for at least part of the day and may not see all you wish. If you enjoy the pomp and ceremony of festivals then the week of Semana Santa is a good time to go although accommodation will be more expensive in the city. Check online to confirm the festival's dates as they vary from year to year.

- Visit a tourist office as soon as you can on arrival to pick up details of attractions and opening times together with a free map which is essential in order to get your bearings and understand where places are located. Tourist offices can be found at the Santa Justa railway station, the Plaza del Triunfo near to the Cathedral and on the Paseo de las Delicias just before the Glorieta los Marineros roundabout in the former Costurero de la Reina building. Hotels usually have free maps and other information for their clients.

- Do your research and read through this guide in order to decide which museums or other places you want to go into before leaving home. Seville has some excellent museums that reflect its history and cultural heritage. Many are closed on Mondays so it is worth checking the opening times. There will also be variations depending upon the time of year.

- Seville has some wonderful places to take refreshment and try a range of Andalusian specialities. While it is wonderful to sit and enjoy a drink or meal in the busy plazas next to top attractions this can be expensive. You will find some good quality tapas bars, cafes and restaurants off the main streets. Ask your hotel where the locals eat for the best deals.

- There are many attractions in Seville and paying for each separately can prove extremely expensive if you want to visit most of them. One option is to buy the *Seville Card* which gives you a pass that can be used on three consecutive days. However, you do need to consider what attractions you want to visit and compare prices to see if this is good value for you. If you are a pensioner there is often a reduced rate for entry. Passes bought online need to be validated when you arrive in Seville so you are probably better to do your research then ask in a tourist office about the pass.

- You will see much more and absorb the atmosphere of Seville if you are able to walk from one place to another but there are a number of options if you wish to take public transport. Although there were originally grand plans for a number of different metro lines the original project was cancelled and at the present time Seville has just one line although it serves a number of stations and carries a lot of commuters. However, it may not cover the areas that you wish to visit.

- Seville has an extensive bus network that does serve all areas of Seville. There are circular buses, C3 and C4 that follow the ring road around the old centre and one, the C5, that takes a circular route inside the centre. They run from early morning to late at night. Each single trip is very reasonable. A cheaper option is to buy the *Tarjeta Multiviaje* which can be bought with a refundable deposit. This can be recharged as you need it and can also be used on the tram. It is also possible to buy a one or three day travel card.

- The tram leaves the Plaza Nueva and travels south. It has four stops and a ticket can be bought from the machine on the platform. This is probably a good option if you just want to experience a tram ride.

- Another option is to use the Hop on Hop off bus that has twelve stops at different points of interest together with an audio guide. You can get on and off as many times as you wish but for a one or two day pass this is an expensive way to travel.

- If you are fit and enjoy cycling it is possible to rent a bicycle to travel around Seville. With its one hundred and twenty kilometres of cycle lanes and two hundred and fifty docking stations you should in theory always be able to find a bike to use. You can get a short-term pass for a week but be aware there is a really hefty deposit.

- There is also the option of taking a boat trip on the River Guadalquivir and seeing Seville and its monuments from a different perspective. The views of towers, castles, elegant bridges and other buildings can be spectacular and also romantic if you wish to take a sunset cruise.

- If you are interested in Flamenco live shows are held regularly. The Casa de la Memoria on Calle Cuna has a traditional flamenco show each evening. In the Santa Cruz district in Calle Ximénez de Enciso you can enjoy a superb show around a horseshoe shaped stage that does not use microphones at the Casa del Flamenco. Another venue in the Santa Cruz district is Los Gallos on the Plaza of Santa Cruz. This show is more expensive than others but lasts longer and offers a variety of traditional and authentic music and dance. The Casa de la Guitarra in Calle Mesón del Moro is a very small intimate location but you need to reserve your seats here. There are also shows every evening at the Museo del Baile Flamenco in Calle Manuel Rojas Marcos.

- Although many people do not agree with bullfighting it is still possible to watch a bullfight in Seville. Purchasing tickets can be difficult as the tickets are only generally released a few weeks before the fights and they sell very quickly. Although the seats in the sun are much cheaper and the performances are in the evening remember that the stone seats have all day to get hot and can still be uncomfortable in the evening. The best way is to book your tickets online before your trip. Use a website that shows a plan of the seats and choose those most suitable for your budget.

# The Tours

# The First Tour

Today's tour begins in the Plaza del Triunfo where you can pick up a map of Seville together with other information from the tourist office. It includes a visit to the Alcázar, the Murillo gardens and the old Jewish Quarter of Santa Cruz then a walk along the eastern bank of the River Guadalquivir to visit the bullring before ending the tour at the famous Market Barranco. You can either walk to the Plaza del Triunfo or take any bus numbered 23, 25, 26, 30, 31, 33, 34, 40, 41, or 42 which stop on Constitution Avenue, not far from the Plaza del Triunfo.

## Main Sights

- Plaza del Triunfo
- Real Alcázar de Sevilla
- Monumento a Cristóbal Colón
- Jardins de Murillo
- Plaza de los Refinadores
- Plaza de Santa Cruz and Los Gallos
- Casa de Murillo
- Convent of San José del Carmen
- Centro de Interpretación Judería de Sevilla
- Hospital de los Venerables
- Plaza de Doña Elvira
- Plaza de la Alianza
- Hospital de la Caridad
- Teatro de la Maestranza
- Plaza De Toros De La Maestranza
- Mercado Lonja Del Barranco

# Plaza del Triunfo

The Plaza del Triunfo, or Square of Triumph, found in the old town of Seville is where the Plaza de los Reyes and the streets of Ceferino González, Joaquín Romero Murube, Santo Tomás and Miguel de Manara all converge.

The square has two monuments and is bordered by Seville Cathedral, the Real Alcázar and the Archivo de Indias. All of these are on the UNESCO World Heritage List. There are also the buildings of the Casa de la Provincia and the Convento de la Encarnación.

### Templete del Triunfo de Nuestra Señora del Patrocinio

The Plaza takes its name from the *Temple of Triumph of Our Lady of Patronage* monument with the image of the Virgin and Child inside. It was built in 1756 to commemorate the survival of Seville after an earthquake the previous year and stands in front of the Archivo de Indias.

*Plaza del Triunfo*

## Monumento a la Inmaculada Concepción

The monument to the Immaculate Conception, constructed by Lorenzo Coullaut Valera in 1918, stands in the centre of the square on its tall white columns. It has an image of the Virgen of Immaculate Conception on the top. The statues of Juan de Pineda, Bartolome Esteban Murillo , Miguel Cid and Martínez Montañés stand at its base. These famous citizens of Seville were advocates of immaculism.

## Archivo de Indias

The Archive of the Indies is housed in what was once the *Casa Lonja de Mercaderes*, the Merchants' Exchange of Seville. It was built in 1572 as the Archbishop was unhappy with the way the merchants used the stairs and interior of the cathedral for their stalls.

The Renaissance building was designed by Juan de Herrera. Today it is a repository that covers around three centuries of history with documents related to the Spanish colonies that include the Americas as well as the Philippines. The Archive of the Indies was created in 1785 by Carlos III. It is possible to visit both its permanent and temporary exhibits.

## Casa de la Provincia

The House of the Province of Seville dates back to the fourteenth century and was originally the headquarters of the Delegation of Seville, known as *Casa Palacio*. It formed part of the Hospital of our Lady of Pilar, the Hospital del Rey and the Hospital Real. It was originally a hostelry for pilgrims but then a refuge for the needy.

The two storey building stands around an elegant rectangular patio with galleries on the ground floor supported on arches held up by Tuscan white marble while the upper floor has high balconies looking out onto the courtyard.

*Walk west on Plaza del Triunfo with Seville Cathedral behind towards Calle Miguel Mañara and the entrance to the Alcázar, the Puerta del León, will be directly ahead.*

# Real Alcázar de Sevilla

The Alcázar is regarded as one of the most beautiful palaces in Spain and has a history covering more than one thousand years. It was originally developed by Moorish Muslim kings as a palace on the site of a tenth century fort and was named Al-Muwarak.

In the thirteenth century the palace was converted to a Gothic style structure then in the fourteenth century King Pedro had it expanded and rebuilt in the Mudejar style. It has outstanding examples of this Mudejar architecture fusing Muslim and Christian buildings. The royal family still use the upper floors as their official Seville residence making it the oldest European royal palace still in use.

### La puerta del León and Patio del León

The entrance to the Royal Alcázar of Seville is through the *Puerta del León*, the Lion's Gate. The name is derived from the nineteenth century inlaid tilework above it that depicts a crowned lion holding a cross in its claws. The lion was a sign of royalty. This gate leads to the *Patio del León*, the Lion Patio which was the garrison yard of the original Al-Muwarak palace.

### Sala de la Justicia and Patio del Yeso

The Hall of Justice, which is just off the Lion Patio, is part of the original Muslim palace. It is one of the most ornately decorated

*Intricate Plasterwork in the Alcázar*

rooms and features an *artesonado*, a ceiling of interlaced beams with decorative insertions. Built in the 1340's by King Alfonso XI it has beautiful Mudejar plasterwork.

Leading from the hall is the *Patio del Yeso*, the Yeso Courtyard, which was built on the home of the Governor of the Caliph of Cordoba in the tenth century and is one of the few buildings that remain from the Almohad period. The patio has a pool in the middle surrounded by myrtle bushes that were grown for their aromatic qualities.

## Patio de la Monteria

The Patio of Hunting is also accessed from the Lion Patio by turning left by the wall that has three arches. This is where the king met the huntsmen who accompanied him on the hunt. The rooms on the western side of the courtyard were part of the Contracting house or *Casa de la Contratación* where trade with Spain's American colonies was controlled.

## Salón del Almirante

The Admiral's room can be found on the right hand side of the Patio de la Monteria. The walls of the room are painted simply in white but from them are hung paintings from the nineteenth and twentieth centuries depicting historical events and characters of the Spanish monarchy. A collection of ornate fans can be seen in the room off its northern end.

A large painting covers the whole wall behind the table that is today used for official meetings. It shows the inauguration of the Ibero-American Exhibition in 1929 that was organised to try to restore Spain's prestige during the reign of Alfonso XIII.

## Sala de Audiencias

The House of Listening or courtroom was also part of the *Casa de la Contratación*. It has an intricately carved wooden ceiling made from sixteenth century gilded boxes. Tapestries hang from the walls with representations of the shields of Spanish admirals and also the painting of the *Virgin of the Navigators* by Alejo Fernández.

## El Palacio Mudéjar or Palacio de Pedro el Cruel

The Mudejar Palace or Palace of Peter I, also known as Peter the Cruel, stands in the Patio de la Monteria. It was built in the mid fourteenth century by craftsmen from Toledo, Granada and Seville. Much of the decoration has been influenced by the Alhambra Palace of Granada. The Palace was completed adding elements from other buildings, mainly from Granada and Cordoba.

The facade of the palace is decorated in Mudejar style and is considered to be the most beautiful part of the Alcázar. The central door is framed by arches that are capped by stucco tracery. Look out for the coat of arms of Castile and León; the castle for Castile and the lion for León.

The palace is divided into two parts; one for official life and the other for private occasions. From the lobby the Patio of Maidens can be reached from the left and the Patio of Dolls from the right.

### Puerta Principal and Patio de las Doncellas

Visitors first pass through the Principal door into the lobby that leads to the *Courtyard of the Maidens*. This was the main courtyard of the palace. Legend states that the Moors demanded one hundred virgins every year as tribute from their Christian kingdoms in Iberia.

The courtyard was at one time paved with white marble surrounding a fountain in the centre but this has since been removed in order to restore the original garden design with its reflecting pool. Built between 1369 and 1379 this elegant courtyard is an excellent example of Islamic architecture with impressive arches depicting open arabesque work above the marble columns.

*The Courtyard of the Maidens*

## Sala de los Embajadores

The Hall of Ambassadors is the oldest of the rooms leading from the Patio de las Doncellas and was the original *qubba,* one of the main rooms of the palace. Entering through a large arch the original doors made in 1366 can still be seen with their carved wood pine leaves and Arabic inscriptions. Inside the inscriptions are in Castilian.

As well as the horseshoe arches inside the square room supported by marble columns with capitals of different colours the room has a magnificent dome of gilded wood built by the carpenter Diego Ruiz dating from 1427. Look out for the detailed work on the walls above the tiles and the Peacocks' Arch that separates this hall from the Peacocks' Hall.

## Patio de las Munecas

The Patio of Dolls is smaller than the Courtyard of the Maidens and was the private part of the palace. It is said to derive its name from the tiny faces carved in the stucco inside some of the courtyard's arches. The patio is surrounded by four galleries. The columns here come from the destroyed palace of Medina Azahara in Cordoba and date back to the Caliph times. The upper floor was added later in the nineteenth century.

## Jardines de las Real Alcázar

The Alcázar has the largest late-medieval European gardens, the most original representation of the Mudejar style. They have undergone continual transformations from their Moorish origins, most significantly during the Renaissance period and reign of Phillip III.

The gardens are divided into separate sections each with a unique style. They are terraced with palm trees, orange trees, lemon trees and other lush vegetation as well as beautiful fountains and pavilions with recessed seats. Although the gardens to the east were created much later in the nineteenth century they are well work a visit.

The first garden, the Garden of the Pond, is really a reservoir placed higher than the other gardens. It has a statue of the god Mercury sculpted by Diego de Pesquera and cast by Bartolome Morel in 1576. The reservoir is surrounded by railings decorated with lions, shields and balls. All were originally gilded but only tracings of the coating now remain.

Behind the reservoir is the *Gallery of the Grotesque* constructed on the old Almohad wall that now has an elevated walkway with wonderful views over the Alcázar buildings, gardens and Cathedral. The walls depict exotic birds and mythological figures painted by Diego de Esquivel while the upper gallery is decorated with crenulations.

From here there are many ways to explore the other gardens. Look out for the *Jardín de la Danza*, the Garden of the Dance; *Las Damas*, the Garden of the Ladies; *El Rústico,* the Rustic Garden; *Jardín de los Ingleses*, the English Garden; the *Jardín de los Poetas,* the Poet's Garden and the Alcoba vegetable garden.

*The Gallery of the Grotesque with the statue of Mercury*

### Puerta de Apeardo and Patio de Banderas

Leaving the Alcázar gardens visitors pass through the rear door or *halt* and the Patio of Flags, said to have derived its name from the flags that were unfurled here to honour important visitors to the Alcázar and where their carriages were kept. From this courtyard there are views of Seville Cathedral and the Giralda.

*Walk east on Plaza del Trifuno for 65 metres then turn right to stay on this road. After 40 metres turn left onto Calle Joaquín Romero Murube bearing a slight right onto Plaza del Patio de Banderas after 7 metres. After 120 metres turn right onto Calle Juderia. Walk for 62 metres then left towards Calle Vida. Turn right onto Calle Vida and bear left after 25 metres onto Calle Agua. Continue for 140 metres.*

## Callejón del Agua

The Callejón del Agua was once the route along which water ran to the Alcázar. In the city wall besides the small alley two pipes that brought water from the *Canos de Carmona*, an old Roman aqueduct, to the gardens can be seen. It was also once the home of Washingon Irving, the American writer.

*From the Calle Agua turn right onto Plaza Alfar. Take the stairs to Calle Antonio el Balarin. After 110 metres turn right onto Paseo de Catalina de Ribera. Walk for 60 metres before turning left and left again. Monumento a Cristóbal Colón will be ahead.*

## Monumento a Cristóbal Colón

The monument to Christopher Columbus sculptured by Lorenzo Valera Coullaut stands in the heart of the Catalina Ribera gardens. Locally it is often referred to as the *Lion Fountain* because a Lion sits on the top of the monument. Look out for the medallions of Christopher Columbus and the shield of the Catholic Monarchs near the base.

## Jardins de Murillo

The Murillo gardens cover an area of 8,500 square metres and are located between the streets of Santa Cruz, the Alcázar and the Catalina de Ribera. Once they were the Alcázar vegetable gardens but in 1911 King Alfonso XIII gave this land to the city.

The gardens were originally called the *Gardens of Talavera* after the architect who designed them but the name was later changed to the Murillo gardens after they were dedicated to the painter Bartolome Esteban Murillo. In 1923 a *glorieta*, or roundabout, dedicated to the painter José García Ramos was built in the centre of the gardens.

*Walk north towards Calle de Nicolás Antonio and cross. Keep walking in the same direction through the Murillo gardens until you meet Calle Cano y Cueto. Turn left then continue onto Plaza de los Refinadores on the right.*

## Plaza de los Refinadores

Separated from the Murillo gardens by a simple iron gate this is a shady square surrounded by low houses. In the centre of the square is the Don Juan Tenorio monument built in 1975. In one corner of the square is the Luis Prieto house that was built between 1915 and 1919. Designed by Anibal Gonzalez it is one of the most fascinating examples of Regionalism in Seville.

*Walk south-west on Plaza de los Refinadores for 45 metres then turn left onto Calle Mezquita. Plaza de Santa Cruz will be seen after 55 metres. Los Gallos is to the south-west of the Plaza.*

## Plaza de Santa Cruz and Los Gallos

When Ferdinand III of Castile freed Seville from Muslim rule he concentrated the Jewish population in this part of the city. It was known as *Juderia* and was a walled area encompassing much of the barrio of Santa Cruz. Seville had the biggest Jewish community in Spain.

*The Consulado de Francia, Plaza de Santa Cruz*

After the Jews were expelled from Spain the area declined until it was revived in the eighteenth century. The square was the site of one of the Jewish quarter's three synagogues. It was later converted to the church of Santa Cruz but then destroyed by the French in 1811. In one corner of the square a plaque states that the church was the burial place of the artist Bartolomé Murillo.

The square is shaded by orange trees and has a small raised garden. In the centre is the *Cruz de la Cerrajería*, the Locksmith's Cross, which is a metal structure that once stood on the corner of Calle Cerrajería and Calle Sierpes. Look out for the small figures and serpents on the top corners.

In the corner of the square there is the mustard yellow building of Los Gallos where some of Seville's most prolific flamenco shows are held. Inside the walls are covered with photos of Flemish paintings and photos of famous flamenco dancers.

*Walk north on Plaza de Santa Cruz and turn left onto Calle Santa Teresa. You will pass the Casa de Murillo and Convent of San José del Carmen. After 130 metres turn right onto Calle Ximénez de Enciso. The Centro de Interpretación Judería de Sevilla will be seen after 50 metres.*

## Casa de Murillo

The House of Murillo was the home where the painter Bartolomé Esteban Murillo lived in the later years of his life. It can be seen at number 8, Calle Santa Teresa and is a two storey building with columns built around a central courtyard that was fashionable and typical of Seville at the time.

Much of the building was taken over by the Andalusian Council of Culture in 1982 but a part was used to create a small museum and art gallery with a seventeenth century feeling.

13

## Convent of San José del Carmen

The Convent of Saint Joseph of Carmen was founded by Saint Teresa in 1575. The church has a single rectangular nave covered by a barrel vault with lunettes while the main chapel is square and covered with a hemispherical dome.

Several important pieces of art are held here. The altarpiece of Jeronimo Velasquez was made in 1630. Look out for the image of the *Immaculate* and *San José with the Boy* by Juan de Mesa as well as *Santa Teresa de Jesus* by Fray Juan de la Miseria.

## Centro de Interpretación Judería de Sevilla

The Jewish Interpretation Centre is a small museum that offers an insight into the lives of the Jews who lived in this area until the late fourteenth century when their homes were confiscated and their synagogues closed. There are stories of the pain and sadness they suffered, their forced conversions, loss of possessions and fate suffered at the hand of the Inquisition.

There are other items such as the leather scroll in which the Jews hid their true beliefs known as a *megillah,* the *mezuzah* which was a parchment for blessing their house as well as a *hannukah* lamp and items used in a *kidush* ceremony. Traditional ceramics and handicrafts with Jewish motifs can be bought in the gift shop.

*Walk south-west on Calle Ximénez de Enciso towards Calle Don Carlos Alonso Chaparro for 110 metres and continue onto Pasaje de Vila for 12 metres. Turn left onto Calle Jamerdana then after 90 metres turn right onto Plaza Venerables and right again after 20 metres. The Hospital de los Venerables will be ahead.*

## Hospital de los Venerables

The Hospital of the Venerable Priests is a seventeenth century Baroque building founded by Justino de Neve and once a residence for priests. The building comprises two parts. The first is the house built by Leonardo de Figueroa. It has a typical Seville courtyard with stunning tiled galleries arranged in a circle that leads to a fountain.

The second section is a church built in 1689 and dedicated to San Fernando. It has a half-barrel vault with beautiful lunettes and arches. Look out for the wall painting in the presbytery vault by Valdés Leal and the works on the high altar by Lucas Valdés and Virgilio Maltoni. There are sculptures by Pedro Roldán and the reliefs are the work of Martínez Montañés.

In 1840 the hospital became a textile factory but then, after complaints, it returned to being a home for the priests. Today after being restored by the Focus-Abengoa Foundation it holds a collection of Spanish paintings and sculptures as well as being a venue for concerts, seminars and temporary exhibitions.

*Walk south-west on Calle Gloria for 30 metres and continue onto Plaza de Doña Elvira.*

## Plaza de Doña Elvira

The small elegant square of Doña Elvira with its orange trees, terraces, tiled benches and fountains is only accessible by foot. Built between 1911 and 1918 it was designed by the architect Juan Talavera y Heredia. Typical Sevillian buildings surround the square and there are restaurants and gift shops here.

In the seventeenth century a famous open air comedy theatre was located on the site. Legend says that the house of Don Gonzalo de Ulloa, the father of Doña Elvira, was situated here giving the square its name.

*Walk north on Plaza de Doña Elvira to join Calle Rodrigo Caro, a narrow zig-zag street named after the poet Rodrigo Caro. After 90 metres turn right onto Plaza de la Alianza.*

## Plaza de la Alianza

The charming Square of Alliance was originally called *Consuelo* or Comfort Square. In the sixteenth century it was known as the *Plaza del Pozo Seco* or Dry Well Square. The old wall runs along one side of the square and a simple fountain stands in the centre. From the square there is a magnificent view of the Giralda and the Convento de la Encarnación.

*Walk west on Plaza de la Alianza to join Calle Joaquín Romero Murube. After 140 metres turn left onto Calle Miguel Mañara then right after 20 metres onto Calle Santo Tomás. Walk for 180 metres then turn right onto Calle Santander. Continue for 180 metres before turning right onto Calle Temprado. The Hospital de la Caridad will be on the right after 65 metres.*

## Hospital de la Caridad

The Charity hospital founded in 1674 is one of the finest examples of seventeenth century architecture and art. The hospital itself still cares for the infirm and elderly but the chapel is open for public visits and contains some wonderful Baroque sculptures. The façade of the church San Jorge, has three levels, the upper two decorated with tiles depicting Faith, Hope and Charity. It is topped by an attic with an iron railing and two brick pinnacles. Inside there are beautiful paintings although today some are reproductions. Look out for the altarpiece by Berna Pineda and the sculptures by Pedro Roldán.

In the main courtyard there are galleries supported by columns and in each of the two courtyards a marble fountain with sculptures representing Mercy and Charity. There is a rear open courtyard with flowerbeds and a high central column crowned by a bust of Miguel de Manara, the founder of the hospital.

*Hospital de la Caridad*

*Walk south on Calle Temprado for 80 metres then turn right onto Calle Núñez de Balboa. Continue for 110 metres then turn right onto Paseo de Cristóbal Colón. The Teatro de la Maestranza will be on the right after 65 metres.*

## Teatro de la Maestranza

The Maestranza theatre is an opera theatre located besides the Alphonse XIII Canal. It was built in 1987 and designed by the architects Aurelio del Pozo and Luis Marín on the site of an old artillery arsenal. It is a cylindrical building with a pediment on top of the old portico. The dome is coloured with red, blue and white stripes.

*Walk north-west on Paseo de Cristóbal Colón for 220 metres. The Plaza De Toros De La Maestranza will be on the right.*

## Plaza De Toros De La Maestranza

The Bullring of the Royal Cavalry in Seville is the oldest bullring in Spain and considered to be one of the finest. It was built and adapted between 1762 and 1881 under the guidance of a number of architects and has an impressive Baroque façade. The *Puerta del Príncipe*, the Prince's Gate, is the main entrance with its beautiful sixteenth century iron gates. They were made by Pedro Roldán but originally belonged to a convent.

The bullring has a small museum that charts the bullring's history from the eighteenth century to the present day with its collection of paintings, posters, bullheads and costumes. If you want to attend a bullfight it is probably best to research the dates when you will be in Seville and book your tickets online.

*From the front of the bullring walk north-west on Paseo de Cristóbal Colón for 270 metres then continue onto Calle Arjona for 65 metres. The Mercado Lonja Del Barranco will be on the left. A perfect place to end the tour!*

## Mercado Lonja Del Barranco

The old Barranco market is an interesting metal structured building located next to the Puente de Isabel II. Originally designed to host Seville's fish market it was built in 1883 and known as the *Naves del Barranco*, or Ship's market.

The building was designed by Gustave Eiffel and has glass walls with high ceilings. The present food market opened in 2014 and today twenty market stalls offer a wide variety of food that includes gourmet tapas. There are a number of different areas to sit both inside and out that include river facing views and terraces from where food and drinks can be ordered directly from the tables.

*Depending upon where your hotel is located you may wish to walk back along the river. If you do want to then walk south-east towards Puente de Isabel II and continue onto Paseo de Cristóbal Colón. Turn right onto Paseo Alcalde Marqués del Contadero then left onto Paseo Alcalde Marqués del Contadero.*

# The Second Tour

Today's tour begins at the Plaza de la Contratación. It includes the spectacular Plaza España, the Parque de Maria Luisa and many of the stunning buildings created for Ibero-American Exhibition of 1929 as well as a number of museums and other interesting places. The tour ends at the Torre del Oro next to the Guadalquivir river. You can either walk to the Plaza de la Contratación or take any bus numbered 23, 25, 26, 30, 31, 33, 34, 40, 41, or 42 which stop on Constitution Avenue, not far from the Plaza de la Contratación. Make sure you ask for the stop nearest the Plaza de la Contratación as this is a long road.

## Main Sights

- Plaza de la Contratación
- Hotel Alfonso XIII
- Real Fabrica de Tabacos
- Plaza Don Juan de Austria
- Plaza España
- Parque de Maria Luisa
- Plaza América
- Museo de Artes y Costumbres
- Museo Arqueológico De Sevilla
- Consulado de Colombia
- Pabellón Argentino
- Pabellon de Guatemala
- Costurero de la Reina
- Pabellón de Chile
- Pabellón De Uruguay
- Casa de la Ciencia
- Teatro Lope de Vega
- San Telmo Palace
- Torre del Oro

## Plaza de la Contratación

The Square of Recruitment, known locally as the Hiring Square, is a small square flanked on one side by the House of Trade, one of the most important historical buildings in Seville. Once the ship captains, trading with the Indies and Flanders came to this square to hire sailors for their ships. Today it is a semi-pedestrian square dotted with orange trees.

*Walk south-east on Plaza de la Contratación for 25 metres then turn left onto Calle San Gregorio. After 130 metres turn left onto Puerta de Jerez and continue onto Calle San Fernando. The Hotel Alfonso XIII will be on the right after 55 metres.*

## Hotel Alfonso XIII

The spectacular Hotel Alfonso XIII is an historic hotel built between 1916 and 1928 specifically for the Ibero-American Exhibition of 1929. It was designed by the architect José Espiau y Muñoz. The hotel was officially opened on April 28 1929 with a luxurious banquet attended by King Alfonso XIII and Queen Victoria Eugenie of Battenberg.

Designed to attract the prestigious and wealthy the building was inspired by Arab architecture and created in the neo-Mudejar style. The façade is spectacular and the interior with its arches and columns, azulejos, hanging lamps, marble floors and carpets from the Royal Tapestry factory exquisite. With its six banqueting halls and inner courtyard the hotel is well worth a visit even if you cannot afford to stay there!

*Walk east on Calle San Fernando towards Calle Doña María de Padilla for 30 metres. The Royal Tobacco Factory will be on the right.*

## Real Fabrica de Tabacos

The Royal Tobacco Factory is now part of the University of Seville. With its eighteenth century industrial architecture it is one of the oldest factories preserved; a magnificent building and well worth a visit. It was built on the site of an ancient Roman burial ground in 1728 by military engineers from Spain and the Netherlands. Surrounded by a moat and sentry boxes it did not come into use until 1757. At the time it was the second largest building in Spain.

Inside the factory there are paintings of the women cigar makers who worked there. Look out for the painting by Bonzalo Bilbao. Originally only men were employed but as demand increased women were employed and were able to make better quality cigars when rolling the leaves. There are free tours of the factory or you can hire an audio guide.

*Walk south-east on Calle San Fernando for 90 metres then turn right onto Avenida el Cid. You will see the Plaza Don Juan de Austria.*

## Plaza Don Juan de Austria

The Plaza of Don Juan of Austria is located at the convergence of the Streets of San Fernando, Carlos V, Cid and Menendez Pelayo. In the middle of the roundabout is the Fountain of the Four Seasons which takes its name from the sculptures of Spring, Summer, Autumn and Winter that surround the fountain. It was built in 1929, the work of Manuel Delgado Brackembury.

*Leave the Plaza Don Juan de Austria and continue for 190 metres along Avenida el Cid until you reach the roundabout. You will see the statue of El Cid and also the attractive building of the Consulate of Portugal as you walk.*
*At the roundabout take the third exit onto Avenida Isabel la Católica and walk for 300 metres. Turn left towards Calle Plaza España for 10 metres, right for 12 metres then left for 38 metres. The Plaza de España will be ahead.*

## Plaza España

The impressive Spanish Square, created by Aníbal González, was completed in 1928 for the Ibero-American Exhibition of 1929. Work was originally begun in 1914 but when Aníbal González resigned in 1926 Vicente Traver completed the work. The plaza is a spectacular example of Regional architecture, using exposed brick, wrought iron and ceramics to blend Renaissance Revival and neo-Mudejar. The building has been the scene for a number of well-known films including *Lawrence of Arabia.*

The building with its central body and two lateral arms is curved, symbolizing the embracing of Spain with its former colonies. At each end of the building are the north and south towers, each seventy-four metres high, linking the network of galleries that run between. If you have the opportunity climb up the north tower for a splendid view in the late afternoon. Built of brick and decorated with marble the building has a gabled roof covered with Arabic tiles.

*Plaza España*

Against the curved arms in alphabetical order there are superb tiled alcoves with benches and tiled walls dedicated to the forty-eight Spanish provinces. Inside each there are maps of the provinces together with the shields of each capital and relevant information and historical facts.

In front of the building the oval plaza covers two hundred square metres. At its edge runs a canal that is crossed by four bridges representing the four ancient kingdoms of Spain; *Castile, León, Aragón and Navarra.* The *Vicente Traver fountain* stands in the middle of the square.

*After visiting the Plaza España walk south-west on Calle Plaza España to explore Parque de Maria Luisa.*

# Parque de Maria Luisa

The park of Maria Luisa is Seville's main public park and has many magnificent buildings, interesting monuments, ceramic tiled benches, fountains and ponds. The gardens originally belonged to the San Telmo Palace but Princess Maria Luisa d'Orleans donated them to the city of Seville in 1893. The park was designed by Jean-Claude Forestier between 1911 and 1914 then in 1929 Seville hosted the Ibero-American Exhibition in the grounds.

Many of the spectacular pavilions built have now become museums, cultural institutions or government offices. Information and directions for some of these attractions can be found below but if you can do try to spend time exploring the park after visiting the Plaza de España. Try to explore the Plaza América and Museo Arqueológico de Sevilla last in order to follow directions for the Consulado de Columbia and rest of the tour. If possible try to pick up a map so that you can find your way around the park.

### Glorieta de Bécquer

The circular Bécquer monument is one of the main attractions in the Park of Maria Luisa due to its composition and beauty. At its centre stands a large tree and around it there is a marble monument dedicated to the romantic poet Gustavo Adolfo Bécquer designed by the sculptor Lorenzo Valera Coullaut. Look out for the marble sculpture of three women clustered to one side who represent different states of love.

### Estanque De Los Lotos

The Lotus Pond takes its name from the aquatic plants that grew in the original primitive garden. The rectangular pond has a stone fountain and is surrounded by pergolas covered with vines and other plants.

**Plaza América**

The American Square, like so many other buildings in Seville, was designed by Aníbal González for the Ibero-American Exhibition of 1929. It is a beautiful square with flowerbeds and a pond in the centre. Surrounding the square are three former pavilions, each with a different architectural style.

The *Pabellón Real* or Royal Pavilion is located to the north of the square and is a flamboyant example of Gothic style completed in 1916. Today it is used for the Town Hall offices.

The *Museo de Artes y Costumbres*, the Museum of Arts and Traditions, is located to the west and housed in the spectacular Mudejar Pavilion designed by Aníbal González as an art pavilion. Today the collection has ceramics, clothing, jewellery, embroidery and musical instruments. Temporary exhibitions are also held here.

To the east is the *Museo Arqueológico de Sevilla*, the Archaeological Museum, housed in yet another of Aníbal González's creations, the Pabellón del Renacimiento, the

*Plaza America*

Renaissance Pavilion. One of its famous exhibits is the El Carambolo treasure discovered in Camas that comprises golden bracelets, a golden chain and pendant and other jewellery. There are also Roman artefacts that include mosaics, statues and busts of famous emperors.

*After visiting the Parque de Maria Luisa and Plaza América walk south-west on Plaza América and turn left onto Paseo de las Delicias. After 120 metres the Consulado de Columbia will be on the right.*

## Consulado de Columbia

The Consulate of Columbia is located in the Columbian Pavilion on the corner of the Paseo de las Delicias where it meets the Avenida Molini. It won the award for the best American example and is the only pavilion still held by the original country that built it. Designed by the Sevillian architect Jose Granados de la Vega it was inspired by neo-Colonial religious architecture. Look out for the *chibchas* and *quimbayas* motifs created by the Colombian sculptor Romulo Rozo.

*Walk back north-west on Paseo de las Delicias and you will see the entrance to the Jardines De Las Delicias. To reach the next part of the tour you can either continue along this road or walk through the gardens until you reach the Glorieta Buenos Aires.*

## Pabellón Argentino

Standing on the Glorieta Buenos Aires you have a good view of the Argentinian Pavilion located in the Arjona Gardens which is today the School of Dramatic Art and Dance. The unique building was created by Martin Saint Noel in a neo-Baroque style with colonial elements.

*From the Glorieta Buenos Aires walk north-west for 40 metres to join the Paseo de las Delicias again. Almost immediately on the left will be the Pabellon de Guatemala.*

## Pabellon de Guatemala

Although small the Art Deco Pavilion of Guatemala with its blue and white tiles is still stunning. The tiles represent the colour on the Guatemalan flag. Look out for the colourful exotic bird the quetzal that is the symbol of Guatemala and Mayan culture. Today it is also part of the School of Dance.

*Continue along Paseo de las Delicias for 250 metres and you will reach the Glorieta los Marineros. The Costurero de la Reina, now a tourist office will be seen opposite on the Paseo de las Delicias.*

*If you are interested in visiting Seville's aquarium turn left just before this roundabout onto Avenida Santiago Montoto and follow the signs. It will take about 10 minutes to walk there.*

## Costurero de la Reina

The building known as the *Sewing Queen* is found next to the Mariners' Roundabout on the edge of the former San Telmo Palace gardens. Designed by the architect Juan Talavera and Vega and built in 1893 it is said to have been the first neo-Mudejar style building in the city, later copied for the Ibero-American Exhibition of 1929. Today it is used as a tourist office.

*After passing the tourist office continue north-west on Paseo de las Delicias for 230 metres then turn right onto Calle la Rábida. Walk for 12 metres then turn right onto Avenida de Chile. The Pabellón de Chile will be on the left after 35 metres.*

*Costurero de la Reina*

## Pabellón de Chile

The rose-red coloured Pavilion of Chile was designed by Antonio Mauricio Cravotto Schiavon and is today part of Seville University. It is said the architect wanted to contrast the coast of Chile with the Andes Mountains and so used a contrast of colours as well as incorporating a tower into the building.

*Walk east on Avenida de Chili for 35 metres. The Pabellón De Uruguay will be on the left.*

## Pabellón De Uruguay

The Uruguay Pavilion was also designed by Antonio Mauricio Cravotto Schiavon for the Ibero-American Exhibition of 1929 and today is part of the University of Seville. Its main façade is on the Avenida de Chile while its rear façade faces the Paseo de las Delicias. The architecture is a mixture of Creole, Colonial and European with neo-Baroque ornamentation.

*Walk south-east on the Avenida de Chile for 110 metres. The Casa de la Ciencia will be on the left.*

## Casa de la Ciencia

The House of Science Museum occupies the former Peru Pavilion, built for the Ibero-American Exhibition of 1929. The beautiful building is attributed to Manuel Piqueras Cotolí. The museum has both permanent and temporary exhibitions as well as a twenty-three metre diameter dome that is equipped with a digital projection system. A range of live astronomy sessions for different age groups are held here.

*Walk south-east on the Avenida de Chile for 20 metres then turn left onto Avenida de Maria Luisa. Walk for 140 metres. The Teatro Lope de Vega will be on the left.*

## Teatro Lope de Vega

The small Lope de Vega theatre is housed in the former *Casino de la Exposicón*, the Casino of the Exhibition, built in the Baroque style for the Ibero-American Exhibition of 1929. It forms part of a larger group of buildings that include a grand ballroom and a central circular lounge with a dome eighteen metres in height. The beautiful buildings are worth a visit just to look at the architecture but the theatre also hosts a variety of shows and concerts that include flamenco, jazz, opera, theatre and dance.

*Continue along this road until you reach Calle de Uruguay then turn left. After 70 metres turn left onto Calle Palos de la Frontera and continue for 400 metres. Turn left onto Avenida Roma. The Palacio San Telmo will be on the left after 80 metres.*

# Palacio San Telmo

The Palace of San Telmo was originally a school for navigators, constructed in the seventeenth century. It is a spectacular building with its elaborate ornamented Baroque portal, designed by Leonardo de Figueroa and his son Antonio Matias. It has large sculptured columns with statues on each side of the balcony that represent the arts and sciences. At the top level, framed by an open arch, there is a statue of Saint Telmo flanked on the left by Saint Hermenegild and on the right by Saint Ferdinand.

The Palace is one of the most beautiful buildings in Seville. The rectangular palace has four towers and a large central courtyard. The main façade is embellished with twelve statues depicting important historical Sevillian characters such as Murillo, Velázquez and Rodrigo Ponce de León. They were sculptured by Antonio Susillo and positioned in 1895.

When the school closed in 1847 it was bought by Antoine d'Orleans, the Duke of Montpensier, who made it into a palace. In 1893 Princess Maria Luisa d'Orleans donated the extensive gardens to the city of Seville and today they form the Maria Luisa Park.

*San Telmo Palace with its ornamental Baroque portal*

*From the Palacio San Telmo walk south-west for 40 metres then turn right onto Paseo de las Delicias. Walk for 180 metres along the edge of the Jardin de Cristina then turn left and then right onto Paseo Alcalde Marqués del Contadero. The Torre del Oro will be on the right after 140 metres.*

## Torre del Oro

Next to the Puente San Telmo is the Torre del Oro or Golden Tower which is a remnant of the original fortified walls built by the Moors to enclose the city. The fortified walls had fifteen gates and one hundred and sixty-six towers. The Golden Tower, dating from around 1220, was a watchtower built to guard the docks of Seville by the Almohad Caliphate.

The tower was one of the anchor points for the chain that stretched across the River Guadalquivir. The lower part was dodecagonal and originally decorated with golden tiles, a mixture of mortar, lime and pressed hay. The two upper parts of the tower are circular and were added in the eighteenth century.

Today the tower houses a naval museum but it is also worth climbing to the top of the tower for the stunning views over Arenal, Triana and the river itself. The nearby *Torre de la Plata,* the Silver Tower, located in Calle Santander is believed to have been built around the same time.

*If you wish to extend the tour you could walk along the river or cross the Puente de San Telmo to explore the more modern area on the other side of the river. If you turn left after crossing the bridge there is a Carriage Museum to visit.*

*Torre del Oro*

# The Third Tour

Today's tour begins in the Plaza Virgen de los Reyes and ends at El Rinconcillo, the oldest Tapas bar in Spain. It includes religious buildings such as Seville Cathedral, convents and churches as well as palaces, museums, plazas and other interesting places that give you an insight into the architecture and atmosphere of this part of Seville. You can either walk to the Plaza Virgen de los Reyes or take any bus numbered 23, 25, 26, 30, 31, 33, 34, 40, 41, or 42 which stop on Constitution Avenue. Make sure you ask for the stop nearest Seville Cathedral and walk along Calle Fray Ceferino González for 100 metres before continuing onto Plaza del Triunfo for 150 metres then onto the Plaza Virgen de los Reyes.

**Main Sights**

- Plaza Virgen de los Reyes
- La Giralda
- Palacio Arzobispal
- Plaza de Santa Marta
- Catedral de Santa María de la Sede
- Plaza del Cabildo
- Arco Del Póstigo
- Plaza de San Francisco
- Plaza Nueva
- Ayuntamiento de Sevilla
- Plaza and Iglesia del Salvador
- Casa de los Pinelo
- Iglesia de San Alberto
- Museo del Baile Flamenco
- Iglesia de San Isidoro
- Casa de Pilatos
- El Rinconcillo

# Plaza Virgen de los Reyes

The Square of the Virgin of the Kings is a beautiful iconic plaza located between Seville Cathedral and the Barrio Santa Cruz. It is dominated by Seville Cathedral and the Giralda bell tower. The Archbishops' Palace and Convent of the Incarnation are also located here. In medieval times this was the *Corral de los Olmos*, the Courtyard of the Elms, where important people met to discuss religious and political affairs.

### Torre de la Giralda

The Giralda tower on the west side of the square was built in the twelfth century as a minaret for the mosque that stood here but in Christian times was converted into a bell tower for Seville Cathedral. In the sixteenth century the current bell tower and its four storeys were added. At one hundred and three metres tall it was the tallest building in Seville for over eight hundred years.

Look out for the weather vane on top of the tower with a statue of *El Giraldillo* that gives the tower its name, meaning *he who turns*. Climb up to the bell chamber to enjoy the spectacular views and see Seville Cathedral's Gothic details. Access is by thirty-five gently sloping ramps that were designed so that those who called the faithful to prayer could climb to the top mounted on donkeys or horses.

### Fuente de la Plaza Virgen de los Reyes

The Fountain of the Virgin of the Kings stands in the centre of the square and was created by José Lafita Diaz in 1925 for the Ibero-American Exhibition of 1929. The grotesques from which the water flows are replicas of the Roman ones found in the *Casa de Pilatos*. The fountain has a Baroque streetlight in the centre.

### Palacio Arzobispal

The Archbishops' Palace is located to the north of the square and dates to the sixteenth century. In the seventeenth century the Baroque façade and lavishly decorated portal were added. Inside the main hall is imposing and the palace, still used by the clergy, has a number of important works of art including a painting by Murillo.

### Convento de la Encarnación

The Convent of the Incarnation was founded in 1591 by Augustinian nuns and located to the south of the square. It was built on the grounds of the fourteenth century Santa Marta Hospital. It is still known as the Hospital of Santa Marta. The main white Mudejar style façade has been well preserved and faces the Plaza Virgen de los Reyes but the old building can also be seen from the Plaza Santa Marta. The building has a tower dating from the twelfth century which was possibly part of the old Almohad defence system.

It is possible to visit the church and its exquisite chapel but not the convent. There are eighteenth and nineteenth century works of art held here, some brought from other convents. Look out for the *Adoration of the Shepherds* by Francisco Dionisio de Ribas.

*The Giralda viewed from the Alcázar Gardens*

*Walk to the south-eastern corner of the Plaza where it meets Calle Mateos Gago. The narrow Barreduela or alley Santa Marta that leads to the Plaza Santa Marta starts here and twists under an overpass that links houses on both sides of the street.*

## Plaza Santa Marta

The tiny square of Saint Martha is hidden and missed by many tourists. It takes its name from the old Santa Marta hospital. In the centre there is a simple stone cross by Diego de Alcaraz that was taken from the San Larazo hospital dating back to 1564 but only placed here in the early twentieth century. The peaceful square has tiled benches and orange trees whose scents fill the air mixed with jasmine and bougainvillea. The door to the right leads into the Convent of the Incarnation.

*Walk back along the alley and turn left onto Plaza Virgen de los Reyes. Seville Cathedral will be straight ahead.*

## Catedral de Santa María de la Sede

Seville Cathedral, *Saint Mary of the See,* is the largest Gothic cathedral in the world and the third largest of all other cathedrals. It was built to portray the wealth of the city which had become a major trading centre after the Reconquista.

Seville Cathedral was built between 1401 and 1506 on the site of the twelfth century Aljama mosque. The only remaining parts from the Moorish dynasty are the *Patio de los Naranjos,* the *Puerta del Perdon* and the *Giralda*. The central nave of the cathedral is forty-two metres high and there are eighty side chapels leading from it.

The *Capilla Mayor*, the Great Chapel, has an enormous Gothic altarpiece that comprises forty-five carved scenes from the life of Christ as well as Santa Maria de la Sede. It is the work of Pierre Dancart, one of the finest examples of Gothic woodcarving and said to be the largest and richest altarpiece in the world.

The *Capitular* or Chapter House has a superb domed ceiling mirrored in the marble floor decoration. There are paintings by the famous artist Murillo. The treasury is housed in the *Sacrista Mayor*, the Great Sacristy. The keys presented to Fernado by the Moorish and Jewish communities on the city's surrender are held here.

Seville Cathedral has fifteen doors on its four sides. The main cathedral door, richly decorated and well preserved, is on the western side and known as the *Door of Assumption*. On this side also look out for the *Door of Baptism* which depicts the baptism of Jesus and the *Door of the Nativity* with sculptures representing the birth of Jesus by Pedro Millan.

*Seville Cathedral*

The door of *Saint Christopher* can be found on the south side while the Gothic style *Door of the Conception* which leads to the *Patio de los Naranjos* is only opened on festival days. This door is on the site of the former prayer hall of the mosque.

The *Door of the Lizard* which also leads from the Patio de los Naranjos takes its name from the stuffed crocodile that hangs from the ceiling. This was a gift from the Sultan of Egypt to King Alfonso X asking for the hand in marriage of his daughter Berenguela.

The *Door of Sanctuary* framed by Corinthian columns leads to the sanctuary while the *Door of Forgiveness* is another way to access the Patio de los Naranjos. On the eastern side is the Door of the *Adoration of the Magi* as well as the *Door of the Bells*.

### Tumba de Christopher Columbus

Although other cities have claimed they have the remains of Christopher Columbus recent DNA tests have proven beyond doubt that the tomb of Christopher Columbus in Seville Cathedral does hold the original remains of the great explorer who sadly died in poverty in Vallodolid.

The tomb which is just inside the cathedral door dates from 1892 and is held up by four allegoric figures representing the four kingdoms of Spain during his life; Castile, León, Aragon and Navarra. It was designed by Maruro Melida and was originally installed in Havana.

### Puerta del Perdon and Patio de los Narnajos

The Door of Forgiveness is a monumental gate that stood at the centre of the old Mosque. It has been restored but has some original bronze plate decoration with two large knockers that are copies of the original Almohad ones. The door gave access to the Courtyard of Oranges from Calle Alemanes. Pilgrims used to come to Seville Cathedral at the end of their pilgrimage. When they passed through the door their sins were forgiven so giving their journey a meaning and purpose.

The Courtyard of Oranges is a legacy of the Almohad mosque and provided a cemetery, ballroom and location for cultural events for the Moorish community. Worshippers would have washed their hands and feet in the fountains here. The central fountain has a basin of the Visigoth period while in the eastern part there is the stone pulpit from where many famous people were said to have preached.

*From the Puerta del Pardon turn left and walk along the cathedral walls to the Avenida de la Constitución. Turn left then walk for 160 metres before turning right onto Calle Almirantazgo. After 60 metres turn right again to stay on Calle Almirantazgo. Continue onto Plaza del Cabildo.*

## Plaza del Cabildo

The Cabildo Plaza is a small semi-circular square that is reached by walking through the surrounding buildings. It has three entrances that are closed at night. It is worth a visit to see the semi-circular building on one side designed by the architect Joaquín Barquín Barron. It consists of a series of arches that are decorated with frescoes and supported by marble columns. To the right is part of the original Almohad inner wall while in the centre is a circular fountain.

The market held here on Sundays is well worth a visit for its stamps, archaeological remains, minerals, coins, medals, military insignia and other curiosities.

*Plaza del Cabildo*

From the Plaza del Cabildo walk south on Calle Almirantazgo for 45 metres then turn right to stay on this road. The Arco Del Póstigo will be straight ahead after 45 metres.

## Arco Del Póstigo

Also known as the *Postigo del Aceite* the Gate of Oil is located near to the *Royal Dockyards of Seville* and is one of the three preserved gates that gave access to the city of Seville. The other two are the *Puerta de la Macarena* and *Puerta de Córdoba*. Built in 1107 and renovated in 1572 by Benvenuto Tortello it was the gate where oil entered into the city. In the twelfth century it was known as the *Gate of Boats* because boats were built nearby. Over the centuries it has had many names, each attributed to the produce that passed through it.

Look above the arch to see the carved stone that depicts Saint Ferdinand and the bishops Isadore and Leander. Inside the arch the rails that once supported the planks used when the river flooded can be seen.

*From the arch walk back eastwards along Calle Almirantazgo for 120 metres to the Avenida de la Constitución. Turn left and walk north for 350 metres then turn right and continue for 90 metres until you reach Plaza de San Francisco.*

# Plaza de San Francisco

San Francisco Square is one of the oldest parts of Seville and by the sixteenth century the square was already well established as a place of government, the location of the Inquisitions' *autos da fe* and a venue for bullfights. The prison where Cervantes was held is also in the square. There are several buildings in this square that are important for their historical, cultural or social interest.

### Ayuntamiento de Sevilla

The back of the City Hall overlooks the Plaza de San Francisco but has its main façade on the Plaza de Nueva. Built in the fifteenth century by Diego de Riano it is an exceptional example of Plateresque architecture. The façade of the building, designed to look like silver, has heraldic shields together with historical and mythical reliefs that depict characters said to be linked to the city such as Hercules, Julius Caesar and the Emperor Carlos.

The building has undergone changes since it was originally built. The new main neo-Classical façade faces the Plaza Nueva. The elaborately carved archway at the southern end of the building was the old main door of the convent.

### Antigua Audiencia

The present building of the Royal Court was built between 1595 and 1597 although there was a house on the site where justice was administered before this time. The building has been renovated a number of times. After parts were destroyed by a fire in 1918 the building was remodelled by Aníbal González in 1923.

It underwent a major renovation in the 1970's when it became the headquarters of the Cajasol Foundation which holds a collection of sculptures, paintings and prints from previous centuries as well as work from contemporary artists. The building has an interesting entrance hall and an elegant central courtyard surrounded by galleries of arches with a fountain.

### Casa de Miguel Arcenegui

The House of Arcenegui was designed by José Espiau and built in 1911. The three storey building uses dark colours for the lower two levels of the façade and white for the remainder. It exhibits a transition style between Modernism and Regionalism. The balconies on the second floor have rounded corners and the arches of the smaller upper windows are decorated with dragons and cherubs. The central body of the house has a neo-Gothic stone cresting with four torch shaped pinnacles.

### Banco de España

The building of the Bank of Spain has a narrow side facing the Plaza de San Francisco and the main façade on Constitution Avenue. Designed by Antonio Illanes del Rio in 1919 the main façade has a shield over the door supported by two lions.

### Edificio de la barra Laredo

The beautiful Bar of Laredo has its main façade on Plaza San Francisco. Designed in 1918 by Ramón Balbuena and Huertas and modified in 1927 by Manuel Cuadrillero Saez the building has five storeys and is a splendid example of Sevillian Regional architecture. It is a unique building with its moulded brick, balconies, wooden viewpoints, railings and tiles.

### Casa de Maria Cháfer

The small but elegant House of Mary Cháfer is one of the first examples of Regionalism. It was designed by the architect Juan Talavera y Heredia and built in 1914.

*Walk to the southern end of Plaza de San Francisco, turn right then walk to the junction of the Avenida de la Constitución and Calle Plaza de San Francisco. Turn right onto this road then walk for 40 metres before bearing right to stay on Plaza de San Francisco. After 15 metres turn left onto Plaza Nueva.*

# Plaza Nueva

The New Plaza is lined with trees and located at the top of the Avenida de la Constitiucion where the *Convento Casa Grande de San Francisco* stood between the years 1270 and 1840. The convent and its gardens originally covered a huge space which extended well beyond the area covered by the square.

The plaza has changed its name over the years according to the passing of different historical events. It was known as *Plaza de la Infanta Isabel*, *Plaza de la Libertad*, *Republic Square* and also *Plaza de San Fernando* but locals called it Plaza Nueva because it was created long after most other places in Seville. During excavations for the Seville metro the remains of a Viking ship were found under the square.

There are a number of interesting buildings surrounding the square. On the eastern side is the eighteenth century façade of the City Hall. This is a good area to stop for sustenance as there are a range of good tapas bars nearby.

*Plaza Nueva*

## Capilla de San Onofre

The small chapel of Saint Onofre is the only part of the convent of San Francisco that remains. It is an excellent example of Baroque architecture and dates back to the sixteenth century. The chapel itself has a single nave covered by a barrel vault with arches and lunettes.

The chapel has four altarpieces. From the seventeenth century there is one by Bernardo Simon de Pineda with sculptures by Pedro Roldán, another named *Animas and the Virgen de la Candelaria* and one dedicated to *San Laureano*. The fourth was commissioned in the sixteenth century for San Onofre. Other things worth seeing are the relief of the Trinity and the *Virgin of Guadalupe* by Juan Correa.

## Edificio Telefónico

The Telefonica building is next to the chapel of San Onofre and was designed in 1926 by Juan Talavera y Heredia. It is an excellent example of neo-Baroque regionalism that was inspired by other fine Baroque buildings in the city such as the churches of Saint Louis and San Pablo as well as the San Telmo palace.

With its elaborate ornamentation and two coloured facades combining grey carved stone with ochre-red brick it should not be missed; especially as it has a viewpoint three storeys high above the building that reminds one of the Giralda.

### Estatua del Rey Fernando III

The equestrian statue of King Fernando III, also known as San Fernando who was declared a saint by the Catholics, stands in the centre of the square to commemorate his victory when the city was won back from the Moors in 1248.

The monument is of neo-Gothic style with the bronze statue standing on a large pedestal surrounded by four stone sculptures, characters who accompanied the king in the conquest of Seville. Around the monument the ground is paved with attractive granite and marble.

### Hotel Inglaterra

The Hotel Inglaterra at one end of the plaza stands on the site of the convent's vegetable garden. Its wonderful original façade was removed in the 1970's but the roof garden offers good views over the plaza and surrounding buildings.

### Edificio Banco de Bilbao

The Bank of Bilbao building stands in one corner of the plaza and dates from 1950. Designed by Galnares Sagastizábal it is four storeys high with tiered facades dominated by six majestic columns.

### Casa Longoria

The neo-Baroque Longoria House was designed by Vicente Traver y Thomas and built between 1917 and 1920 for Don Miguel García de Longoria. The symmetrical façade uses a light-coloured brick together with blue tiles for detail. It is three storeys high with a French window and covered balcony above the entrance. On the corner of the building rises a beautiful viewpoint tower.

*Walk to the north of Plaza Nueva and turn right onto Calle Grandada. After 80 metres turn left onto Calle Francisco Bruna. Continue for 35 metres then turn right onto Calle Entre Cárceles and walk for 45 metres. Turn left onto Calle Álvarez Quintero then after 40 metres turn left onto Plaza del Salvador.*

# Plaza del Salvador

Saviour Square takes its name from the *Iglesia del Salvador*, the Church of Saint Saviour which is located here. The busy square is used as a local meeting place. In the eleventh century it would have been a souk surrounding the mosque and part of the square was used as a cemetery until the sixteenth century.

In the Middle Ages part of the square was used as a water store from the *Canos de Carmona*, the Roman aqueduct that bought water to the city. Little changed until the mid-nineteenth century when it was remodelled.

### Iglesia del Salvador

The Church of the Saviour is the largest in Seville after the Cathedral. Built on the site of the Ibn Adabbas mosque and completed in 1712 it stands with its magnificent Baroque rose-pink façade on the east side of the square. Many artists including José Granados and Leonardo de Figueroa were involved in its building.

The base of the belfry is part of the former mosque minaret while the middle Gothic part with two open windows on each side was added in the fourteenth century. The magnificent Baroque top was added in 1718. It is still possible to see the original *Courtyard of Prayer* belonging to the old mosque.

Inside the church are three naves with small chapels to the sides. The main nave has a barrel vault and the transept is covered with a dome topped by a lantern. Behind the altar is a small museum with its collection of paintings and other objects of art. With stunning architecture and the wealth of its collections, including fourteen altarpieces, the church is well worth a visit.

### Hospital de la Paz

The hospital of the Lady of Peace standing opposite the Iglesia del Salvador is also an interesting Baroque church constructed in the sixteenth century. Hospital buildings have been on this site since the fourteenth century. The building comprises three storeys with two bell towers on the top. The first level has four semi-recessed Doric columns.

The building is arranged around a central courtyard with open galleries enclosed with arched columns. The second level has smaller columns in the central zone with rich decorations of angels and other figures together with sculptures of Saint Augustine, Saint John and the Virgin. The third level has a central window framed by pilasters.

### Monumento a Martínez Montañés

This monument is dedicated to the famous sculptor Juan Martinez Montanes. Made from bronze it depicts the artist sitting down, holding a chisel and an image of the Immaculate Conception while creating the image of the *Ciguecita*, one of his most famous works.

*Walk to the south of Plaza del Salvador and turn left onto Calle Blanca de los Ríos. Walk for 65 metres then turn right onto Calle Francos. After 70 metres turn left onto Calle Pajaritos and continue for 120 metres. Turn right onto Calle Estrella and almost immediately left onto Calle Bamberg. Walk for 50 metres then turn left onto Calle Abades. Casa de los Pinelo is 2 metres ahead.*

## Casa de los Pinelo

Located at number fourteen Calle Abades the House of Pinelo was built in the early sixteenth century for Don Diego Pinelo, the canon of Seville Cathedral. Considered to be one of the most important noble houses in Seville the Renaissance house belonged to the Pinelo family until 1524 when it was donated to Seville Cathedral and continued to be used by the cathedral canons until the nineteenth century. Today it houses the Seville Royal Academy of Fine Arts and the Santa Isabel Hungary Royal Academy of Fine Arts.

*Courtyard Casa de los Pinelo*

The beautiful corner mansion is two storeys high with a combination of Italian Renaissance and Mudejar architecture. The house has two patios with many of the main rooms arranged around the *Patio of Honour*. Look out for the beautiful Corinthian columns, the Carrara marble and the exquisite Moorish plasterwork. In the other courtyard there is the statue of the goddess Pomona.

The panelled wooden ceilings are beautiful and the walls hung with wall paintings. The grand staircase leads to the top of the house with its coffered ceiling, galleries and an exhibition of Japanese and Chinese art. These are but a few of the many things the house has to offer.

*Walk back to Calle Bamberg and turn right. Continue for 22 metres then turn right onto Calle Argote de Molina. After 35 metres bear left onto Calle Manuel Rojas Marcos. The Iglesia de San Alberto will be on the left after 15 metres.*

## Iglesia de San Alberto

The church of Saint Albert is part of a monastery complex originally occupied by the Carmelites who founded it in 1602. The church itself dates from the eighteenth century and is all that remains of the convent. The exterior has a high brick façade with an entrance door flanked by Tuscan pillars framing the semi-circular arch. The slim tower topped with a spire has blue and white tiles. It is best viewed from further along Calle Estrella.

The church has a single nave with side chapels on both sides, an attractive dome and an altarpiece. A variety of artwork can be enjoyed including the sculpture by Angel Iglesias called the *Crucificado del Perdón*, the Crucified of Forgiveness.

*Walk north on Calle Manuel Rojas Marcos for 25 metres and the Museo del Baile Flamenco will be on the right.*

## Museo del Baile Flamenco

The Museum of Flamenco Dance is housed in the four storey eighteenth century *Casa de Palacio*, the Palace House. As you wander through the building enjoying the exhibits from the past as well as modern technology you will experience the magic of flamenco and understand its attraction.

A typical Andalusian courtyard can be found on the first floor and in the basement arched brick passageways lead to the old cellar where workshops and recitals are still regularly held. The first floor has the costumes and memorabilia associated with flamenco while the second floor has an exhibition of works by Vicente Escudero.

*Walk north on Calle Manuel Rojas Marcos for 41 metres. Continue onto Calle Luchana for 60 metres. Turn right onto Calle Augusto Plasencia. The Iglesia de San Isidoro will be on the right after 20 metres.*

## Iglesia de San Isidoro

The church of Saint Isadore was a temple built in the fourteenth century over an old mosque. The church has a mixture of Gothic, Baroque and Mudejar architecture and an unusual façade to its tower. It consists of two parts. The lower has a ceramic panel with the effigy of San Isidoro in the centre and medallions of San

Leandro and Santa Justa on the sides while the top has a semi-circular arch, pilasters, spire and forged cross.

It has three naves and side chapels with ten pillars supporting the arches installed during the Baroque period. There is an impressive Baroque dome and the vault is decorated with murals. The altarpiece in the chancel is by Felipe del Castillo. There are numerous other altarpieces and works of art such as paintings of *Saint Augustine and Saint Monica* as well as *Saint Jerome and Saint Peter* by Francisco Pachero dated 1600. In the Chapel of the Three Falls the tomb of Bishop Gonzalo Herrera can be seen to the right of the main altar.

*Walk south-east on Calle Augusto Plasencia for 50 metres. Turn left onto Calle Cabeza del Rey Don Pedro and continue for 75 metres then turn right onto Calle Águilas and walk for 210 metres. Continue straight onto Plaza de Pilatos for 75 metres then turn left onto Calle Medinaceli. After 34 metres make a slight left onto Calle Imperial. Walk for 60 metres and the Casa de Pilatos will be on the left.*

## Casa de Pilatos

The house of Pilatos is a beautiful civil Andalusian palace built in the sixteenth century that is famous for its magnificent patio and gardens. Although privately owned by the Medinaceli family it is open for public viewing.

The palace has a mixture of Italian Renaissance, Gothic and Mudejar architectural styles and is decorated with glazed coloured ceramic tiles or *azulejos*. The house originally belonging to Don Fadrique Enríquez de Rivera, the first Marquis of Tarifa, was dramatically changed after he was influenced by his visits to Florence, Venice and Rome.

*Principal Patio Casa Los Pilatos*

The entrance to the palace is through a marble gate of Renaissance style designed by Antonio Maria Aprile in 1529 and topped with a Gothic crest. This leads into the *Patio Principal*, the main patio, an Andalusian courtyard which has classical columns, balconies with Gothic balustrades and a Genoese fountain in the centre. The courtyard is decorated with sculptures of Roman emperors and statues from Greek mythology as well as a fountain.

The main patio opens into two attractive gardens. The larger garden was originally an orchard and is lined with open galleries with niches filled with classical statues. In the smaller garden there is a grotto and a pond with a fountain portraying Bacchus.

A tiled stairway, considered to be the most magnificent in Seville, leads to the upper floor apartments and has a Mudejar honeycomb ceiling. You can join a guided tour to visit the furnished rooms and the art collection of the Medinaceli.

Throughout the interior the walls are decorated in detailed Mudejar style and some rooms have elaborate coffered ceilings. In the left wing of the Tower there are frescos on the ceiling by Francisco Pacheco and in the following room works by Francisco Goya and Giuseppe Recco. Paintings by Luca Giordano can be viewed in the library. The chapel is a mixture of Gothic and Mudejar styles and holds numerous manuscripts.

*Walk south-east on Calle Imperial for 22 metres then turn left onto Callejón Calería. After 37 metres turn right onto Calle Juan de la Encina. Continue for 97 metres then turn left onto Calle Santiago. Walk for 350 metres before turning left onto Calle Juan de Mesa.*

*Walk for 60 metres, turn right onto Calle Alhondiga then left after 54 metres onto Calle Gerona. El Rinconcillo will be on the left 15 metres along this road.*

## El Rinconcillo

The Rinconcillo is Spain's oldest tapas bar, first opened in 1670. Visiting this bar is a must because it is like walking back through time. The waiters with their waist-coats and ties charge around serving the crowds that pack into the bar. Dusty bottles line the walls and large Iberico-hams hang from the ceilings.

It is wonderful to watch the waiters carving the ham and then see them chalk the bill onto the wooden bar. This is a good place to end the tour by having a drink and bite to eat while soaking up the atmosphere.

*El Rinconcillo with the bill chalked on the wooden bar*

# The Fourth Tour

Today's tour begins at the Torre de los Perdigones with spectacular views of the city. It explores the authentic and colourful Macarena district with its Moorish walls, the oldest Sevillian market, beautiful palaces, churches, museums and the Modern Mushroom sculpture. Buses 02, A2, C1, and C3 stop in Calle Resolana, C5 in Calle Feria; just a few metres from the Torre de los Perdigones.

## Main Sights

- Torre de los Perdigones
- Hospital de las Cinco Llagas
- Murallas and Arco de la Macarena
- Basílica de la Macarena
- Casa Grande del Pumarejo
- Iglesia de San Hermenegildo
- Puerta De Cordoba
- Iglesia de San Julían
- Monasterio de Santa Paula
- Iglesia de Los Terceros
- Palacio de las Dueñas
- Palacio Marqueses de la Algaba
- Mercado de Feria
- Iglesia de Omnium Sanctorum
- Alameda de Hércules
- Casa de las Sirenas
- Plaza de la Encarnación
- Espacio Metropol Parasol
- Iglesia de la Anunciación
- Palacio de la Condesa de Lebrija
- Museo de Bellas Artes

## Torre de los Perdigones

The Tower of the Pellets was part of the *Buckshot Factory* constructed in 1885 for the manufacture of pellets. The area was run down but around the time of the Ibero-American Exhibition of 1929 it was restored. The tall square brick tower has sections divided by thin ledges that gradually decrease in size. Each part has a hollow middle and a circular window. The top section is surrounded with a metal balcony.

The forty-five metre tower today houses the Camera Obscura. The guided tour which includes experiencing the Camera Obscura gives time to enjoy the spectacular city views and take photographs from a perfect vantage point.

*Walk east on Calle Resolana for 300 metres then continue onto Calle Parlamento de Andalucía for 130 metres. Turn left onto Calle San Juan de Ribera. The Hospital de las Cinco Llagas will be on the left.*

## Hospital de las Cinco Llagas

The Hospital of the Five Wounds is today the Parliament of Andalusia. The building dates back to 1546 as a legacy from Don Fadrique Enríquez de Ribera who wanted to create a new building for the charity founded by his mother in 1500. It was designed by Martín de Gainza who was succeeded in directing the works by Hernán Ruiz II. It is said to have similarities with the large hospital in Milan.

The huge Renaissance building was designed around nine courtyards although only eight remain today. It has long facades divided horizontally into three levels with mouldings and cornice. At the centre of the south façade is a large Baroque style doorway designed by Asensio de Maeda which leads directly to the central courtyard and the hospital's church.


58

The church is built on a Latin-cross design with an altarpiece designed by Diego López Bueno together with paintings by Alonso Vázquez. The large garden is divided into two areas. Look out for the sculpture of Hercules and the towers on the corners of Calle Don Fadrique and Calle San Juan de Ribera.

*Walk south-west on Calle San Juan de Ribera for 160 metres then turn right onto Calle Parlamento de Andalucía. The Murallas de Sevilla, the old city walls, will be on the left.*

## Murallas de Sevilla

The defensive city walls of Seville were built in Roman times but modified and maintained throughout subsequent historical periods until the nineteenth century when parts were demolished. Originally there were eighteen gates but today only the *Puerta de la Macarena*, the *Puerta de Córdoba*, the *Postigo del Alcázar* and *Postigo del Aceite* remain. The wall can be followed along Calle Macarena to the Macarena Gate and Basilica.

*Walk west on Calle Parlamento de Andalucía for 15 metres. Turn left onto Calle Don Fadrique/Calle San Luis and continue for 45 metres. Turn left onto Calle Macarena. The Arco de la Macarena will be on the right after 20 metres.*

# Arco de la Macarena

The Macarena Arch is also known as the *Puerta de la Macarena*. It was the gate used by the kings who visited the city. Although originally Roman and then extended by Ali Ibn Yusuf in the twelfth century it was remodelled in 1723. It is said to take its name from an important Moor named Macarena.

*Walk west on Calle Macarena for 20 metres. The Basílica de la Macarena will be on the right.*

*Puerta Macarena and Basilica de Macarena*

# Basílica de la Macarena

The neo-Baroque Macarena church completed in 1949 is famous for its sculpture of the *Virgen de la Esperanza Macarena*, the Lady of Hope Macarena. In the church's museum the Virgin's jewels and the *Semana Santa* floats are displayed. La Macarena is the patron saint of bullfights and gypsies.

*Walk south on Calle San Luis for 190 metres then turn left onto Plaza Pumarejo. After 30 metres turn right to stay on Plaza Pumarejo. Walk for 20 metres. The Casa Grande del Pumarejo will be on the left.*

# Casa Grande del Pumarejo

The Grand mansion of Pumarejo was built in the late eighteenth century after Pedro Pumarejo demolished over seventy surrounding houses to make room for his grand project. It is a two storey building with Moorish ornamentations that covers over two thousand square metres. The building is arranged around two courtyards, each with very different characteristics.

*Walk south on Plaza Pumarejo for 20 metres. Turn left onto Calle Fray Diego de Cádiz and continue for 230 metres. Turn right onto Calle Morera then after 30 metres make a slight left onto Calle Puerta de Córdoba and walk for 50 metres. The Iglesia de San Hermenegildo will be on the left. Attached to it is the Puerta de Cordoba.*

### Iglesia de San Hermenegildo and Puerta De Cordoba

The church of San Hermenegildo is a seventeenth century temple where Saint Hermenegildo was said to have been imprisoned and executed. The church has a single nave covered by a barrel vault with transverse ribs, lunettes and a dome.

The Cordoba Gate is one of the four remaining entrances to the city. It can be accessed from the church of Saint Hermenegildo. The remains of murals can be seen on the walls.

*Walk south-east on Calle Puerta de Córdoba for 15 metres. Turn right onto Calle de Madre Dolores Márquez. Walk for 60 metres then continue onto Calle San Julián for 100 metres. The Iglesia de San Julián will be on the left.*

## Iglesia de San Julían

The Gothic Mudejar church of Saint Julian was built in the first half of the fourteenth century. After a fire and looting in 1932 the church was rebuilt. It has three naves and a triumphal Gothic arch. The church holds a number of artworks including a sculpture of the Immaculate by Alonso Cano and works by Antonio Castillo Lastrucci.

*Walk south on Calle San Julián for 6 metres. Turn left onto Calle Duque Cornejo. Walk for 28 metres then continue onto Calle Moravia for 50 metres. Turn right onto Pasaje Mallol. Walk for 230 metres then make a slight left onto Calle Santa Paula. After 15 metres the Monasterio de Santa Paula will be on the left.*

## Monasterio de Santa Paula

The Monastery of Saint Paula was founded by Doña Ana de Santillan in 1473 for the Order of Saint Jerome. It has been modified a number of times over the centuries. Today the simple brick Gothic façade is mixed with the Moorish and Renaissance style of the sixteenth century. The slender steeple is very elegant while the sixteenth century portico and Plateresque façade are outstanding.

It has two entrances from the outside. One leads to the museum convent and the Chapel of the Sacred Heart while the other leads to the church. The church was built between 1483 and 1484 and is of Gothic Mudejar design with ribbed vaults that are elaborately decorated and a magnificent coffered ceiling in the nave which is attributed to Diego López de Arenas. It has a number of interesting altarpieces.

There are two cloisters that are interconnected by an arcade of columns and arches. The principal one was extended in the seventeenth century by Diego López Bueno. The museum has a collection of paintings, sculptures and jewellery.

*Walk south-east on Calle Santa Paula for 70 metres. Turn right onto Calle Enladrillada. Walk for 140 metres then turn left onto Plaza San Román. After 33 metres turn right onto Calle Sol and continue for 150 metres. The Iglesia de Los Terceros will be on the left.*

## Iglesia de Los Terceros

The Church of the Third Order of San Francisco is part of a complex of buildings that was originally a convent constructed in the seventeenth century. The other parts are now offices for the water company and a residential building.

The former convent is set around two cloisters and a staircase leading up to an ornate dome decorated with plasterwork. The main cloister is rectangular in shape and has semi-circular arcades supported by marble columns and pedestals with diamonds on the four fronts. The other cloister is square with open galleries. The main staircase is regarded as an excellent example of Baroque Andalusian architecture.

The Baroque church is built as a Latin-cross that has a single nave covered by a barrel vault with lunettes and a spandrel dome on the transept. There are chapels to each side of the nave. The church has five altars and the superb altarpiece by Francisco Dionisio de Ribas covering the main wall of the chancel is one of the best examples of seventeenth century art.

*Walk south-west on Calle Sol for 25 metres then continue onto Plaza los Terceros for 30 metres. Turn left to stay on Plaza los Terceros. Walk for 23 metres then turn right onto Calle Gerona. After 130 metres turn right onto Calle Doña María Coronel and walk for 55 metres before turning left onto Calle Dueñas. The Palacio de las Dueñas will be on the right after 60 metres.*

## Palacio de las Dueñas

The Palace of the Dueñas is the official residence of the Dukes of Alba and was the favourite home of Cayetana the eighteenth duchess who spent much of her life here. While the upper part is the private family residence it is possible to visit the ground floor. It takes its name from monastery of Santa Maria de las Duenas, the site upon which the building stands.

The palace built in the late fifteenth century by the Pineda family was sold in order to recover the husband who had been taken prisoner by the Moors. It comprises a number of buildings and courtyards that mix Gothic, Moorish and Renaissance architecture. Originally the palace had over one hundred marble columns, eleven patios and nine fountains. The beautiful palace is steeped in history and has much to offer. The shield of the Duchy of Alba can be seen on the seventeenth century Tirana tile placed in the arch of the main entrance. In another part of the palace is a plaque that recalls the birth of the Spanish poet Antonio Machado who was born in the palace in 1875.

The Andalusian patio is picturesque and behind the garden is a stunning courtyard enclosed by white marble columned arches. Look out for the Mudejar panel that leads to the *Patio del Limonero* where you will find ceramic jars bearing the name of the palace and also the tower in the corner of the main patio.

There are sculptures, paintings, tapestries, ceramics and furniture by a range of artists as well as bullfighting costumes and memorabilia. One of the main attractions is the decorative art collection containing one thousand four hundred and twenty-five items. As well as the large collection of Spanish paintings from the nineteenth and twentieth centuries there is a watercolour by Jackie Kennedy that was painted during her visit in 1960.

*Walk west on Calle Dueñas for 55 metres. Turn right onto Calle Gerona and walk for 22 metres. Turn right onto Calle Espíritu Santo. After 150 metres turn left onto Calle Castellar. Walk for 35 metres then turn right onto Calle Laurel.*

*Make a slight left onto Plaza los Maldonados after 35 metres. Walk for 20 metres then continue onto Plaza Monte Sión then onto Calle González Cuadrado. Walk for 260 metres to Plaza Calderón de la Barca. The Palacio Marqueses de la Algaba will be on the right after 37 metres.*

## Palacio Marqueses de la Algaba

The Palace of the Marquises of Algaba was built in 1474 by Juan de Guzman, the first Lord of Algaba, although much of the present building relates to the sixteenth century. Completely restored at the turn of the century it is considered to be one of the best examples of civil Mudejar architecture in Seville.

*Façade of Palace of Marquis of Algaba*

The lower part of the two storey building is built from stone blocks while the upper is decorated with tiles. It is arranged around a central courtyard with galleries originally supported with Genoese marble columns although only one now remains. The present building is much smaller than the original one. The old tower with its Gothic lower part and Mudejar style above is integrated into the main façade. It is also possible to see the remains of the great palace staircase and the beautiful coffered wooden ceilings.

The Mudejar Art Centre now housed in the building has a collection of one hundred and eleven items related to the Mudejar artistic style. They include a baptismal font, tiles, tombstones, jars and seals.

*Walk south on Plaza Calderón de la Barca for 4 metres. There will be an entrance to the market on the right.*

## Mercado de Feria

The Feria Market dating back to 1719 is one of the oldest buildings of its kind in Seville although it has since been expanded and modified. It comprises two buildings that are separated by a small alley. As well as the stalls selling flowers, fresh meat, fish and other produce there is a market bar that serves fish and sea food tapas.

*Exit the market to Feria Street. The Iglesia de Omnium Sanctorum will be next to the market.*

## Iglesia de Omnium Sanctorum

The Church of Omnium Sanctorum built in 1249 combines Mudejar and Gothic architecture and is one of the oldest churches in Seville. After an earthquake in 1356 it was repaired and a Gothic chancel added. It was also burned during the revolts of 1931 leaving only the walls and the gates intact.

The main façade has a number of interesting features. Constructed of stone the entrance is flanked by pointed arches and above this is a small richly decorated Mudejar window. There is a large Gothic rose window that lights the main nave and two smaller ones for the aisles. Look out for the small reliefs of human heads on the arch. The square tower is built of brick and still has some of the original windows. It has interesting decorations and is topped by a high spire.

The church has three naves that are sub-divided into five sections, the central one being wider and taller than the others. The building has quadrangular pillars with pointed arches that support the modern Mudejar inspired wooden roof. Look out for the Nave of the Gospel that has interesting chapels leading from it, the Nave of the Epistle, the double ribbed vault of the presbytery, the paintings, statues and numerous altarpieces.

*Walk west on Calle Peris Mencheta for 170 metres then turn left onto Alameda de Hércules, walking for 20 metres before turning right onto Calle Belén. After 33 metres this road turns left and becomes the Alameda de Hércules.*

# Alameda de Hércules

The Mall of Hercules was built in 1574 and was originally the oldest public garden in Europe. It was built upon a swampy area through which the River Guadalquivir once flowed but was turned into a public garden for the people of Seville by the Count of Barajas.

Standing at the entrance to the large square are two huge columns from an ancient Roman temple. One is topped by the mythical founder of Seville, Hercules, while the other has a statue of Julius Caesar who founded Híspalis, the city upon which Seville was established. In the eighteenth century two columns topped by a statue of a lion were erected at the other end of the square. One bears the coat of arms of Seville and the other that of Spain.

Three fountains have been installed in the square. They are surrounded by anti-slip paving finished in blue and white enamel. The fountains send up vertical sprays and misty clouds not only to delight the children but cool the atmosphere too. Today the square is filled with pubs, cafes, tapas bars and clubs. It is a wonderful place to rest and take refreshment.

# Casa de las Sirenas

On the western side of the square is the *Casa de las Sirenas*, known locally as the Mermaid's House. Built in 1861 it was designed in the style of a French eighteenth century palace for the Marquis of Esquivel by the architect Joaquín Fernández Ayarragaray. The house is surrounded by a pink wall and has gates with the same design as the Tobacco Factory. Today the building is owned by the local government and used for cultural activities and as an exhibition centre.

*Walk along the Alameda de Hércules until it meets Calle Amor de Dios then turn right. After 280 metres turn left onto Calle García Tassara. Continue for 52 metres then turn right onto Calle Daoiz. Walk for 110 metres then turn left onto Calle José Gestoso. After 100 metres turn right towards the Plaza de la Encarnación.*

# Plaza de la Encarnación

The medieval Square of the Incarnation is of historical significance. The ancient Roman gate for the northern part of the city once stood here. Later around 1810 when the Augustinian convent was demolished it became a vibrant market and centre of city life. Since then the square has had a number of uses, including that as a car park. During excavations in 2003 the archaeological remains of *Hispania* were discovered here, making it the most important Roman site in the city.

### Espacio Metropol Parasol

In order to transform the Plaza de la Encarnación an international competition was held. It was won by the German architect Jürgen Mayer with his Metropol Parasol. Known locally as *Las Setas*, the Mushrooms, it is made up of six gigantic wooden mushroom-like structures built upon five levels, one of which is underground.

The Parasol with its bars, restaurants, farmers' market and archaeological museum provide a range of activities for locals and tourists. From the top that is thirty metres high there is a spectacular panoramic view of the surrounding area.

*Espacio Metropol Parasol*

### Iglesia de la Anunciación

The Church of the Annunciation was founded in 1565 and completed in 1579. The brick façade is flanked by two Ionic columns. The main door comprises two parts. The lower has an arch with two niches while the upper has three niches. The beautiful relief of the *Virgin with Child* can be seen in the centre with the statues of San Jose and San Rafael to the sides.

The church is built upon the Latin-cross design and has a vaulted ceiling in the main chapel. There is a bell tower and the cupola is decorated with ceramic tiles. In the crypt is the pantheon where many famous citizens of Seville such as Benito Arias Montano and Gustavo Adolfo Bécquer are buried.

Currently the *Faculty of Fine Arts* this church has a wonderful collection of important paintings such as the *Annunciation* by Antonio Mohedano and the *Exaltation of the name of Jesus* by Juan de Roelas. Look out for the beautiful altarpieces especially the ceramic *Christ of the Good Death* and the *Immaculate Conception* which contains valuable sculptures by Juan Bautista Vázquez the Younger.

### Fuente de la Anunciación

The Baroque fountain of Annunciation was made of marble and stood in the former market. It is considered to be the oldest public fountain in Seville that was not merely decorative but there as a public water supply fed by the Roman aqueduct, *Los caños de Carmona*. Look on the side for the inscription with the date and reason for its creation.

*From the Plaza de la Encarnación walk west along Calle Laraña for 130 metres then turn left onto Calle Cuna. After 70 metres the Palace of the Countess of Lebrija will be on the right.*

## Palacio de la Condesa de Lebrija

The Palace of the Countess of Lebrija was built in the fifteenth century but its typical Sevillian façade was added in the sixteenth century. It has since been owned by a number of noblemen who remodelled and extended it. In 1901 it was bought, restored and reconstructed by the Countess of Lebrija, who had a passion for archaeology, in order to house her valuable collection of antiquities.

The palace is known for its collection of Roman mosaics and the first glimpse of these is seen after walking through the Al Andalus archway into the Andalusian open air patio with its Mudejar style arches. The courtyard is paved with an intricate Roman mosaic. More mosaics are seen in other rooms on the ground floor.

As well as these wonderful intricate mosaics the rooms are filled with priceless archaeological treasures such as Greek, Roman, Persian and Etruscan ceramics, vases, sculptures and other relics such as jewellery. Hanging from the walls are paintings and on the upper level are rooms with Arabic and Asian themes as well as the family dining room and library.

*Retrace steps on Calle Cuna then turn left onto Plaza Villasís. Continue onto Calle Martín Villa for 65 metres, Calle Campana for 50 metres, Plaza del Duque de la Victoria for 65 metres and Calle Alfonso XII for 300 metres. Turn left onto the Plaza del Museo and the Museo de Bellas Artes will be about half way down on the right.*

## Museo de Bellas Artes

The Seville Museum of Fine Arts is located in the former seventeenth century Merced Calzada Convent that was built in the Mudejar style by Peter Nolasco in the time of King Fernando III. In the seventeenth century it was remodelled by the Spanish architect and sculptor, Juan de Oviedo y de la Bandera in an impressive Mannerist Andalusian style.

Today the building is arranged around three patios and joined by a large staircase. The patios are decorated with tiles, trees and flowers. It has works from the Gothic period to present times that include an impressive collection of works by Murillo, El Greco, Valdés Leal and Zurbarán.

Even if you do not visit the museum the salmon-coloured façade of the building is worthy of viewing. The doorway is part of the original convent as is the ceiling in one of the main museum rooms. It is also possible to visit the church located at the far end of the museum. Many items of architecture taken from various convents in Seville have been used to decorate its door.

*On leaving the museum there are a number of cafes and places for refreshments in the Museum Square and surrounding streets.*

*The main gate of the Museo de Bellas Artes de Sevilla*

74

# The Fifth Tour

Today's tour explores the barrio of Tirana on the western bank of the Guadalquivir River. The narrow cobbled streets, ceramic workshops and other sights convey an atmosphere different to other parts of Seville yet many tourists never visit this area.

Traditionally it was home to sailors, bullfighters and flamenco dancers who were not originally allowed to live within the main city walls. The *azulejos* or ceramic tiles have been made in the area using mud from La Cartuja, to the north of Triana since Roman times.

The tour begins on the eastern side of the Puente San Telmo then explores the Tirana area before crossing the Puente de la Barqueta back to the eastern bank. If you have a metro station near your hotel the Puerta de Jerez is the nearest stop on this side of the river or the Plaza de Cuba on the Triana side. Otherwise you can take the 03, 21, 40, 41 40, 41, C5 or A2 buses that stop nearby.

**Main Sights**
- Puente San Telmo
- Calle Betis
- La Casa de las Columnas
- Iglesia de Santa Ana
- Capilla de los Marineros
- Corral Herrera
- Iglesia San Jacinto
- Ceramica Triana and Ceramica Santa Ana
- Mercado de Triana
- Plaza Altanzo
- Museo del Castillo De San Jorge
- Capilla Virgen del Carmen

- Puente de Isabel II
- Callejón de la Inquisición
- Iglesia de Nuestra Señora de la O
- La Basílica del Patrocinio
- Torre Sevilla
- Torre Triana
- Torre Schindler
- Pabellón de la Navegación
- Monasterio de la Cartuja
- Jardin de Guadalquivir and Jardin Americano
- Puente de la Barqueta

*Calle Betis*

# Puente San Telmo

The concrete bridge of San Telmo was built between 1925 and 1931 by the by engineer Joseph Eugenio Ribera and named after the San Telmo Palace which is situated nearby. It has been modified over the years and links the older part of Seville with the newer Los Remedios district. Standing on the bridge the San Telmo Palace can be seen to the south and the Torre del Oro to the north.

*Walk south-west across the San Telmo bridge then at the roundabout take the first exit onto Calle Betis. After 220 metres turn left onto Calle Troya then right after 35 metres onto Calle Pureza and the Casa de las Columnas will be on the right.*

# Calle Betis

Betis street runs alongside the river and takes its name from the Roman name for the River Guadalquivir. It is a fascinating street with beautiful eighteenth century brightly coloured urban facades and restaurant terraces with spectacular panoramic views of the Giralda, Torre del Oro and Bullring across the river. Its restaurants, bars and authentic flamenco shows provide a buzzing nightlife.

# La Casa de las Columnas

The House of Columns is today the Civic Centre with municipal buildings and the public library. The main entrance is on Calle Pureza, Purity Street, with a central balcony supported by two Tuscan columns and its year of construction 1789 engraved on the door. It also has a frontage on Calle Betis facing the river. The Baroque style Patio House dating from the late eighteenth century was once home to the University of Merchants and has rooms arranged around two courtyards.

*From the Civic Centre walk north-west on Calle Pureza for 5 metres towards Calle de Vázquez de Leca then turn left onto Calle de Vázquez de Leca. After 21 metres the Iglesia de Santa Ana will be on the left.*

## Iglesia de Santa Ana

Construction for the historic church of Saint Anna began in 1266 at the request of King Alfonso X. Although not a cathedral it is often referred to as the *Cathedral of Triana*, probably because of its beauty and diversity.

The church is of Mudejar Gothic style and was the first Christian church built in this new part of Seville after it was reconquered in 1248. The initial building was heavily fortified. Over the years the church has undergone changes. The original

*Iglesia Santa Ana*

bell tower was demolished in the seventeenth century and replaced. The upper two parts have open arches and coatings of blue tiles. An octagonal spire coated with blue and white ceramic tiles crowns the top.

The earthquake of 1755 seriously damaged the building so it was remodelled by the architect Pedro de Silva who made some significant changes. The outside of the church is a curious mixture of colours and styles with brick and stone being used in its construction. It is decorated with ceramic altarpieces. The outside still retains its Baroque appearance but between 1970 and 1972 some of the church's medieval features were recovered inside.

*From the Santa Ana church walk 21 metres north-east on Calle de Vázquez de Leca. Turn left onto Calle Pureza then walk for 130 metres. The Capilla de los Marineros will be on the right.*

## Capilla de los Marineros

The Chapel of the Mariners was built in 1759 on the site where the Chapel of the College of Merchants once stood. It has had a number of changes over the years, at times being a theatre, a warehouse, an Anglican Church and even a cabaret location. In 2010 it was enlarged and refurbished and today belongs to the Brotherhood of Hope of Triana.

The three storey chapel has an attractive white and yellow façade. In the centre the large door has a niche above with an image of the Immaculate Conception and above this there is a set of three bells.

Inside the chapel has a central nave with two small aisles. The nave of the original chapel has a neo-Mudejar coffered ceiling and an eighteenth century Baroque altarpiece with the image of *Our Lady of the Hope of Tirana*. The nave of Sagrario has a neo-Baroque altarpiece with the *Christ of the Three Falls* which has undergone a number of restorations since its creation in the seventeenth century. In the nave of San Juan Evangelista there is a Baroque eighteenth century altarpiece dedicated to Saint John the Evangelist.

*Leave the Sailors' Chapel and walk south-east on Calle Pureza for 50 metres then turn right onto Calle Torrijos. Walk for 110 metres then continue onto Calle Luca de Tena for 65 metres. Turn right onto Calle Pagés del Corro. The Corral Herrera will be on the right after 60 metres.*

## Corral Herrera

The Corral Herrera is one of the four interior courtyards that remain in Triana. The corrals were old communal patios, known as *corrales de vecinos*, where the *gitano* or gypsy families used to live. There were many rooms around this courtyard which was used not only for cooking and washing but also for singing and dancing.

*Walk west on Calle Pagés del Corro for 240 metres then turn right onto Calle San Jacinto. Iglesia San Jacino will be on the right after 28 metres.*

## Iglesia San Jacinto

The church of Saint Jacinto was built on the site where the chapel of La Candelaria belonging to the old hospital once stood. It was built between 1742 and 1745.

The façade of the church is built from an attractive ochre coloured brick. The main entrance of the church was the work of Matías José de Figueroa. It sits between a semi-circular arch that is topped by a straight pediment and pinnacles. Above the large round window is a beautiful Baroque belfry.

*Walk south-west on Calle San Jacinto for 30 metres then turn right onto Calle Pagés del Corro. After 120 metres make a right turn onto Calle Antillano Campo. Walk for another 100 metres for the Ceramica Triana and a further 75 metres for Ceramica Santa Anna.*

## Ceramica Triana and Ceramica Santa Ana

The barrio of Triana was once home to Seville's tile workshops and potteries that were known throughout the world. Nearly every tile seen in the buildings and gardens of Seville will have been made here. Ceramic workshops are rare now but in July 2014 the Centro Ceramica Triana opened as a museum in the old Santa Ana ceramics factory.

Ceramica Santa Ana, founded in 1870, was the most famous tile shop in Triana. It sells reproduction ceramic ashtrays from the 16th century. You will see other similar shops along this road.

The museum has three areas where you can find out about the industry. On the ground floor are the kilns and raw materials used while on the second floor there are examples of ceramics from the Moorish times up to the late 1950's. There is also a part of this floor devoted to information on the Triana area such as its festivals and flamenco dancers.

*Walk south-east on Calle San Jorge for 130 metres towards the Puente de Isablel II then turn left onto Plaza del Altonzano.*

## Plaza del Altozano

The Altozano square is located in the very centre of Triana. Most of the buildings here were built in the twentieth century. In the square there is a monument to one of the best bullfighters in history, Juan Belmonte. There is also a monument to the art of flamenco. Look out for the Murillo Pharmacy building that was designed by the Regionalist architect José Espiau y Muñoz between 1912 and 1914.

### Mercado de Triana

Triana's main market is built upon the ruins of the old castle of Saint George in the Plaza del Altozano. As well as selling the normal goods associated with a food market it has a sushi and oyster bar, a small brewery and is a venue for performing arts.

*From the Plaza del Altozano walk north-east on Calle Puente de Isabel II and you will reach Museo Del Castillo de San Jorge, Capilla Virgen del Carmen and the Puente de Isabell.*

# Museo Del Castillo De San Jorge

The Museum of the Castle of Saint George is situated next to the north tower of the Triana bridge. Just walk down the steps leading from the street. The museum is actually underneath the market.

*Museo Del Castillo De San Jorge*

The Castle of Saint George was the seat of the Spanish Inquisition and the museum brings to life what living in these times was like. Triana was the area where thousands of people were imprisoned over the centuries. The audio guide with its atmospheric introduction is free. You will see the ruins of the castle and the cells that were often flooded by the Guadalquivir River.

## Capilla Virgen del Carmen

The Chapel of the Virgin Carmen which was completed in 1928 is situated on the west side of the Puente de Isabel II or Triana Bridge and built by the architect Anibal Gonzalez. It is a small chapel built from brick and decorated with Triana ceramic tiles that were designed by Emilio Garcia Garcia.

There are two towers joined by a rectangular middle building. The lower, wider tower is capped with a ceramic dome that has the shield of the Carmelite order and a small temple with green columns. Inside this temple are the sculptures of Santa Justa and Rufina. The other tower which is octagonal in shape is used as a bell tower.

## Puente de Isabel II

The Isabell II Bridge also known as the Triana Bridge was once known as the Bridge of Boats because the people used to cross the river by walking across a line of boats that were tied together.

In the nineteenth century it replaced the old pontoon bridge said to be the oldest in Spain. The bridge was built by the French engineers Gustavo Steinacher and Ferdinand Bennetot between 1845 and 1852 and was the first solid bridge built in Seville.

*From the Puente de Isabel II bridge walk back until you meet Calle San Jorge then turn right and continue for 110 metres. Turn right onto Calle Callao and after 40 metres bear right onto Callejón de la Inquisición.*

## Callejón de la Inquisición

Inquisition Alley is a narrow passage about thirty-five metres long that takes its name from the times of the Inquisition when those accused were either taken along it to the jail in the Castle of Saint George or to their death. The alley is accessed by passing through an arch which is topped with three ceramic pinnacles and reaches the river by small flights of stairs. The gate is locked at night.

*Walk back south-west on Callejón de la Inquisición then turn right onto Calle Castilla. The Iglesia de Nuestra Señora de la O will be on the right after 160 metres.*

## Iglesia de Nuestra Señora de la O

The Church of our Lady of O was built on the site of an ancient mosque. There is some controversy over when it was first built and it has had a number of modifications over the centuries. Antonio Gil Gataón was responsible for the building that took place between 1697 and 1702. Today it is a blend of Moorish, Renaissance and Mannerist architecture.

The façade is Mudejar style and the door is surrounded by a flared pointed arch with archivolts. It has spectacular intricate decoration above that is divided into three parts. On the lower part two shields are supported by lions while the middle has four decorated closed arches. The top part is decorated with a row of small columns topped by an ornamental grid and a roof supported by corbels. The current bell tower was added in 1604 by Alonso de Vandelvira using a Mannerist style. The first part is quadrangular while the second level is elliptical.

The church is quite small with three naves, a presbytery and choir. It is supported by arches on red marble Corinthian columns decorated with plasterwork. In the chancel there is a magnificent Baroque altarpiece dating back to 1630. The church has many other artefacts to enjoy including the Sacramental chapel which is decorated with tiles made in Tirana by Garcia Montalban and the superb carving of Jesus of Nazareth, head of the Brotherhood of the O, by Pedro Roldán in 1685.

*Continue north-east on Calle Castilla for 550 metres. La Basílica del Patrocinio will be on the right.*

## La Basílica del Patrocinio (Cristo del Cachorro)

The present basilica has been formed by two chapels that were built at different times. It is very characteristic of Seville's religious traditions and is well worth a visit.

The older chapel dates from the late seventeenth century and is today the Sacramental chapel that has a Baroque altarpiece taken from the former convent of Carmen. There is also the *Virgen del Patronociniio* and the sculptures of San Isidoro and San Leandro.

Because the church was so small in 2012 a small basilica was added that now forms the new part of the chapel. It has been built from carved brick and is beautifully decorated with ceramic tiles depicting the Virgin, the Passion and death of Christ.

The main altarpiece of carved and gilded wood has a stunning image of *De Cristo de la Expiración,* Christ of the Expiration. It is fondly referred to as *El Cachorro* which translates as The Puppy. Francisco Antonio Gijón is responsible for this image which is regarded as one of the best woodcarvings ever made.

*Walk back east along Calle Castilla for 50 metres then turn left onto Ronda de Triana and slight left again after 12 metres to stay on this road for another 50 metres. At the roundabout take the third exit onto Calle Gonzalo Jimenez de Quesada. Walk for 170 metres then turn right onto Calle Juan de Castellanos and make a left turn after 15 metres onto Calle Inca Garcilaso. The Torre Sevilla will be on the right.*

## Torre Sevilla

The Seville Tower was the first skyscraper to be built in Seville. It is the tallest building in Andalusia and the seventh tallest in Spain. It was designed by Argentine Cesar Pelli and completed in 2015. Built mainly from glass and concrete it has forty-three floors and a roof garden. When it is lit up at night it looks like a torch.

*Walk north on Calle Inca Garcilaso for 95 metres then turn left onto Calle Juan Antonio de Vizarrón. Walk for 12 metres then turn right onto Calle Inca Garcilaso. The Torre Triana will be on the left.*

# Torre Triana

The Triana tower is the largest administrative building in Andalusia. It was built in 1993 having been designed by Francisco Javier Saenz de Oiza who used the Castle Sant Angelo in Rome as his inspiration.

The large round tower has many similarities with the one in Rome although instead of being topped with an angel the one in Triana has two yellow chimneys that refer to the Pillar of Hercules, a symbol of Andalusia. It is used as an exhibition hall and a public administration building.

*Walk north on Calle Inca Garcilaso for 110 metres then turn right onto Calle Jerónimo de Aguilar. After 160 metres you will see Torre Schindler.*

*Torre Sevilla and Torre Triana*

# Torre Schindler

The Schindler Tower, named after its Swiss manufacturer, was a lookout tower designed for the Exposition of Seville in 1992. It is sixty-five metres in height and has eighteen floors. The lift transfers visitors from the ground floor to the upper terrace in twenty-four seconds. From the terrace there is a wonderful view of the River Guadalquivir and surrounding area.

*From Torre Schindler walk north on Camino de los Descubrimientos for 60 metres then turn onto Calle Jerónimo de Aguilar. The Pabellón de la Navegación will be 60 metres along this road on the left.*

# Pabellón de la Navegación

The Navigation Pavilion was built for the Exposition of Seville in 1992 and designed by the Sevillian architect Guillermo Vázquez Consuegra. Dedicated to scientific explorations and discoveries it was one of the most visited pavilions of the exhibition. It has been the home of a navigation museum since 2012.

*From the Pabellón de la Navegación walk north on Camino de los Descurimientos for 150 metres then turn left onto Calle Francisco de Montesinos. After 250 metres turn right onto Calle Américo Vespucio. The Monasterio de la Cartuja will be on the right.*

# Monasterio de la Cartuja

The sixteenth century honey-coloured stone building of the Monastery of Cartuja is surrounded by walls and located on the Isla la Cartuja. The monastery has a spectacular entrance gate and is surrounded by extensive grounds with a lake, a beautiful walled garden where fruit trees grow and a small Mudejar tower. It has a domed church with several chapels, a Mudejar cloister, a crypt and tombs.

The monastery has a rich history that includes visits from Christopher Columbus who stayed here while planning his second voyage and the troops of Napoleon who expelled the monks and used it as a barracks damaging many of the buildings in the process. The monks returned for a short time before it was confiscated in 1830.

The monastery became a world famous ceramics factory when the abandoned buildings were bought by a Liverpool merchant named Charles Pickman. In the late nineteenth century the factory won many prizes for its pieces and numerous commissions were made for Spanish monarchs. When the factory closed it moved its production to Saltereas in the east part of Seville.

Today the monastery holds a contemporary art gallery and is a venue for open-air concerts. There is a café with a wonderful outdoor seating area where one can sit and relax while taking refreshments. It is possible to walk through the attractive tiled factory entrance and see the chimneys and old factory buildings.

*Walk south on Calle Américo Vespucio for 350 metres then turn left onto Calle Francisco de Montesinos before bearing slight left onto Camino de los Descubrimientos. Walk north-east on this road for 1.2 kilometres then turn right onto Matemáticos Rey Pastor y Castro. After 240 metres the Guadalquivir Garden will be on the right.*

# Jardín de Guadalquivir and Jardin Americano

Between the monastery of Cartuja and the Isla Magica theme park are the Guadalquivir and American gardens. Both were built for the Exposition of Seville in 1992 but then fell into disrepair. They have since been refurbished and reopened in 2010.

The Guadalquivir garden is a park with sculptures and themed areas. There are pools filled with water lilies frequented by wild birds with viewing platforms to enable a closer look. There are shady wooded areas, a herb garden, a rose garden, an avenue lined with orange trees and a maze. The American garden is a botanical garden with specimens from the American continent.

 *From the Guadalquivir Gardens walk east on Calle Matemáticos Rey Pastor y Castro for 110 metres then make a slight right onto Calle Matemáticos Rey Pastor y Castro for 35 metres. At the roundabout take the first exit onto Puente de la Barqueta.*

# Puente de la Barqueta

The Bridge of Barges is a suspension bridge that spans the Alfonso XII channel of the River Guadalquivir linking the Isla de Cartuja with the rest of Seville. It was designed by the civil engineers Juan Jose Arenas de Paul and Mark Jesus Pantaleon Prieto and built between 1989 and 1992 for the Exposition of Seville in 1992. The attractive steel arch is two hundred and fourteen metres long and has ends that form a triangular gantry on each side with the board itself being one hundred and sixty-eight metres long. Built on land barges were used to place the bridge in its final location.

*Puente de la Barqueta*

*Cross the bridge and you will be back on the east bank of the river. There are bus stops and cafes in the surrounding streets. It is possible to walk back along the river to the town centre or to explore things you have missed on other days of the tour. Here you are near the Museo de Belles Arts, the Macarena district and other interesting buildings.*

# Final Thoughts

These tours were written in response to guided tours that the author attended whilst in Seville, all of which tended to rush the participants from one location to the next and only included the most popular tourist sites such as Seville Cathedral, the Alcázar and the Plaza España.

The tours have been designed to give you an insight into the way Seville has developed. You will have passed over the remains of the Roman city Hispalis upon which Seville was founded, walked upon an ancient Roman burial ground, seen the defensive city walls and gate, the Canos de Carmona pipes of the aqueduct, the columns in the Alameda de Hercules as well as the Roman mosaics and artefacts displayed in museums.

By visiting the different parts of the city you will have seen the great influence the Moors had upon Seville and how the Arabic style inspired the Christians to create the Mudejar art and architecture. Many of the buildings visited will have provided examples of how Gothic, Renaissance, Moorish, Arabic, Baroque, and Mudejar blend together.

You will also have seen buildings of Mannerist, neo-Classical and Modernist styles and those built for the Ibero-American Exhibition of 1929 influenced by Spanish colonies that blend Colonial, Creole and neo-Baroque. The walks will have demonstrated the skill of architects, builders, sculptors and painters who have made Seville the city it is today.

The importance of religion to many Sevillians will have been evident and there will have been empathy for the lives many experienced in the past, especially during the time of the Inquisition. In addition there will have been the opportunity to see paintings and other great artworks in palaces, museums and churches, enjoy magnificent views or spend more time in favourite locations.

There may not be time to explore the interior of every building or visit all museums included in each day's walking tour so a section for your own notes is included over the next few pages. Here you may wish to make notes of places to visit if you have any spare time on another day, or intend to return to Seville in the future. You may also wish to write down things such as restaurants or favourite attractions that you can pass onto friends.

# NOTES

# Notes

# NOTES

# NOTES

# NOTES

You may also enjoy reading...

A GUIDE TO
VERONA

FIVE WALKING TOURS

P S QUICK

Lightning Source UK Ltd.
Milton Keynes UK
UKHW020642230519
343192UK00008B/81/P